Seventy Light Years

FREDDIE YOUNG

An Autobiography as told to Peter Busby

ff

faber and faber

LONDON·NEW YORK

Peter, thank you for helping me tell my story.
It has not been possible to mention all the wonderful crews with
whom I've worked, but I would like them to know how much
I have appreciated their contribution to my success.

First published in 1999
by Faber and Faber Limited
3 Queen Square London WC1N 3AU
Published in the United States by Faber and Faber Inc.
a division of Farrar, Straus and Giroux Inc. New York

Typeset by Faber and Faber Ltd
Printed in England by Clays Ltd, St Ives plc

© Freddie Young, 1999

Freddie Young is hereby identified as author of this work in accordance
with Section 77 of the Copyright, Designs and Patents Act 1988

A CIP record for this book
is available from the British Library

ISBN 0–571–19793–0

1001522702

T

10 9 8 7 6 5 4 3 2 1

Seventy Light Years

Contents

Foreword

Imagine me on the vast set of *You Only Live Twice* in 1967. I was a lowly 16mm news cameraman, hired for the day by a friend from Swiss TV to grab some shots of this massive James Bond film. I didn't dare turn over during a take. But as the last explosions shook the stage and I heard the director shout 'Cut!', I saw my chance. With hand-held camera whirring, I walked through a smoke cloud and, spotting Sean Connery, moved into a big close-up. It was a terrific effect, but Connery didn't think so – he was furious and, with justifiable anger, tore me off a strip.

I wasn't surprised. People like me had to be prepared for treatment like that – actors and technicians were under tremendous pressure. So when the famous Director of Photography came in sight, my heart sank. It was the great Freddie Young. I admired him so much I didn't want my first encounter to go the same way. So I hid behind my Swiss friend. He approached Young and introduced me, and to my amazement, the sun came out. Freddie Young might have been pruning his roses. He was so relaxed and friendly and charming – where was the stern disciplinarian I had heard about?

He responded to my interest in the silent days by telling me he had started in the film industry in 1917 – in the laboratory at the old Gaumont Studio, Lime Grove. He told me what it was like to tint and tone the old film stock, getting his forearms stained amber or yellow or blue; to edit films and then to have to cut the negative without a solitary key number. I looked nervously around – surely I was holding things up? Freddie Young was the linchpin of such a spectacular film. But you'd never know. He was in his element on the studio floor and he knew exactly what was going on around him without having to look.

When he heard that I knew Charles Rosher, he told me that he had modelled his work on Rosher's, and that of other great American camera-men such as Lee Garmes and George Barnes – all of whom he met when he went to Hollywood just before the war. It was difficult to believe this man was sixty-five – retirement age. (He finally retired twenty years later!) And what an incredibly adventurous life he had had – filming in the Valley of the Kings in Egypt while Howard Carter uncovered Tutankhamen's tomb over the next hill. Doing dangerous stunts for silent pictures. Crossing the U-boat-infested Atlantic to make *49th Parallel* in Canada. Getting blown up while filming for the army. And all this long before his great period with David Lean.

When he had to stop talking to me, he was genuinely apologetic. I was profoundly impressed by the man. And when I decided to devote my life to film history, Freddie Young became one of my most valuable sources of information – always reliable, always sensible, and often surprising. And when I came to write my biography of David Lean, he became a primary contributor and checker of the manuscript. Unlike Lean – who walked out on his wife and son – Freddie was a reassuringly warm family man, as you will discover from his son's tribute at the end of this book.

I'm sure Freddie owed much of his longevity to the devotion of his wife Joan and his son David – both remarkable people. And to have been acclaimed the world's greatest cinematographer, to have been showered with awards, including three Oscars, an OBE and an honorary doctorate from the Royal College of Art, must have been immensely gratifying. But as you'll read in this fascinating book, what kept Freddie going through 96 years and 161 films was that most precious quality for any filmmaker – enthusiasm.

Kevin Brownlow, London, 1998

Freddie Young with some of the fruits of his labour – including three Academy Awards for achievement in cinematography.

Prologue

I was born on 9 October 1902 in a mews cottage in Marylebone, the seventh of eight surviving children.

My mother, Anne Frances Challis, had brought to the marriage a considerable dowry, which my father proceeded to squander. For a time he ran a training stable in Isleworth, but that failed to prosper, so he took us off to the Curragh, a region of Ireland famous for horses. A few months later we were back in Bryanston Mews, Marylebone. My father bought a brougham, a horse-drawn carriage with a collapsible roof for transporting paying customers. It was a smart-looking affair, and he dressed for the part, in a double-breasted blue coat, a top hat with a cockade, with a plaid rug over his knees. I remember going down to the stables to watch him grooming the horses. They gave off one of those smells that stay with you for the rest of your life.

Otherwise we didn't see much of him. Isaac Henry Young, known as Ike, was a handsome man with a big moustache but he was a bit of a roughneck. At night he'd be out drinking, and at the end of the week he would give Mother a sovereign for the housekeeping, which didn't go far among ten people. My mother was a lovely woman, but I don't have very happy memories of my Dad.

My mother had an aunt who lived in Godolphin Road, a respectable area of Shepherd's Bush. We children were often taken over to see 'Aunt' Anne, a tall, stately lady always dressed in black silk. After her death my mother told us she wasn't her aunt at all but her mother. As a young woman in Perthshire Anne had married the younger son of one of the Border earls. Soon after my mother was born he discarded her, which proved not too difficult because a Scottish marriage was not recognized in England, so our mother told us. He paid her off and she lived in comfort for the rest of her life, keeping what to her was the shameful secret of having being deserted. My grandmother was buried in her home town of Lambourn, Berkshire. I went there some years ago to look at her grave, but all I could find was a pile of broken tombstones against a wall.

It was extraordinary for us children suddenly to learn our grandfather had been a baronet, the second son of an earl. There was a feeling in the family that we'd been cheated out of our birthright. I think it's wrong to dwell on such things. It just prevents you from going out and making your own way in the world.

My earliest memory is of wandering out of the house, aged about seven. When I reached the archway at the entrance to the mews there was a man just entering. Around his neck was a strap holding a tray of horse meat and a big knife. This was 'the cat's-meat man', one of many hawkers, like the muffin man, who used to come round selling things. He'd shout 'Cat's meat! Cat's meat!', and those people with cats would buy a pennyworth of meat. That day the man was feeling particularly malevolent; either that or he had a macabre sense of humour. He stopped in his tracks, waved his knife menacingly, and hissed, 'I'll have your gizzard!' I ran home, terrified.

At school too certain teachers took a delight in terrifying children. One of these was Mr Graham, a great big tall man with gingery hair cut short and piercing blue eyes that protruded alarmingly. On the slightest provocation out would come his cane. One morning he entered the classroom and growled, 'You'd better behave yourselves today. I've had vinegar for breakfast.'

Fortunately they weren't all like that. The headmistress at my infants' school was Mrs Mirror – 'Mrs Looking-Glass', we called her behind her back. When I was about eight there was a big royal procession, the funeral of Edward VII possibly, which I was determined to watch. Mrs Looking-Glass was against this, she probably thought we would be trampled on, and we were ordered to stay away. Next day I was on the kerbside, one out of tens of thousands lining up to watch the parade go by. I remember the huge crowds, the flags, colour, excitement, police on their horses . . . Suddenly I felt a tap on my shoulder. In the midst of this multitude Mrs Looking-Glass had singled me out. I was sent home, missing all the fun.

After my grandmother died in 1915, we went to live in her house in Shepherd's Bush, which gave us more space and comfort. She had antique furniture, a davenport and a rosewood sewing table, which I still have, and we installed gas to replace the candles and oil lamps. We would gather round the piano on Saturdays and Sundays and have a singsong. Hearing old music-hall songs always brings back the strongest memories of my eldest sister Violet with her lovely voice, and my brother Bill playing the one-string fiddle he'd made himself out of a cigar box.

Violet was then twenty-six and soon to be married. Lucy and Dora were both dressmakers. George, at nineteen the only one of us to have had a decent education, was a toolmaker. Soon he and Charlie, two years younger, would go to fight in the Great War. Then there were Bill and me and Wyn, still at school. I was fourteen and longing to leave and make my own way in the world.

1 A Huge Greenhouse

I was always mad on films. My brother Bill and I used to go to the local cinema a couple of times a week. There were two features, a cartoon, newsreel and a short documentary known as an 'interest' film. For an afternoon show both of us could get in for three ha'pence. Sometimes we'd stay and see the whole lot through twice, if we didn't get caught. Cinemas in town, like the Empire, Leicester Square, had a full orchestra to accompany silent films, but at our west London local there was just one man thumping a piano. It was there that I first saw Chaplin, the Keystone Cops, Tom Mix the cowboy, D. W. Griffith pictures like *Birth of a Nation,* and my own favourite actress, Mary Pickford.

Near my home in Shepherd's Bush there was this curious building. Large and ugly, with the upper storey made entirely of glass, it reminded me of a huge greenhouse. Bill and I would go swimming in Lime Grove Baths directly opposite, and I always wondered what this place was. Then someone told me it was the Gaumont Film Studio. This set me thinking. How marvellous it would be to work in a film studio. Well, I said to myself, why not try? So one day in 1917 I went down there and knocked on the door.

A man answered, wearing a white coat with mauve edges round the collar. The conversation that followed was like the scene in an old movie when the shy but intrepid hero gets his big break in the world. 'What can I do for you, young man?' he asked. I told him I wanted a job in the film industry. He questioned me, and found out I liked to take photographs with my Kodak Box Brownie. 'Right,' he said, 'you start work tomorrow.'

This wasn't my first job. With my two eldest brothers fighting in the trenches, I'd left school as soon as I could, to help support the family. At fourteen I was too young to join up, so instead I worked in a munitions factory, drilling the tops of hand grenades. I hated the noise and the general atmosphere there, and I only stuck it for a week or two. Various other jobs followed: tinning copper tubes for the radiators of Napier cars, a

The famous Gaumont Studio, in Lime Grove, Shepherds Bush, London (1917).

short stint at the White City splicing ropes for army tents, then a more interesting job at an artificer's guild. An old lady had died, leaving her silver and jewellery to be made up into a chalice. I helped the craftsman to beat the silver into a thin plate and hammer it into shape around a wooden ball, before setting the gold leaf and the rubies and emeralds into the cup. The combination of craft and artistry appealed to me, but not when I had the chance to work in a film studio.

Lime Grove later became the home of BBC Television Current Affairs, but in 1917 it was the British end of Frenchman Leon Gaumont's empire, and one of the most modern studios in the country. In a separate works next door they processed all the Gaumont release prints from America and the rest of the world, as well as the newsreel films from Gaumont Graphic. The main building, where I worked, had two floors. Downstairs was the scene dock, properties and other departments, and the laboratory, and above this, with its walls and roof of glass, the studio.

I now found out the purpose of this greenhouse. It was so they could shoot using natural light. This was a good idea in theory, but in practice it didn't work out so well. If it was a foggy day, which it often was, the studio became a pea-souper. On a cloudy day the cameraman would turn on a few lamps to provide sufficient exposure, then the sun would come out, bathe the set in light, and ruin the shot. The management tried various things to remedy this. They painted the glass green to kill the sunshine, they installed roller blinds, finally they painted the studio black and used only artificial light. And in 1928, after my time, the Ostrer brothers, Isidore and Maurice, bought the company, pulled the studio down and rebuilt it.

The crew on a picture was much smaller then. There was the director, his assistant, the art director (or 'scenic artist', as he was called), a few electricians and stage-hands, the property man, and the cameraman and his assistant. The extraordinary thing was they all wore white coats. They looked like a lot of doctors. I suppose it was thought to be something to do with cleanliness, since we were working with film. Different-coloured stripes around the collar indicated the wearer's position: red for the cameraman, blue for the chief electrician, mauve for the director. Some coats were more elaborate, in expensive silk, with pearls and bits of ribbon – anything to make the man distinctive. I realized I'd been lucky when I first knocked on the door. The man who answered was Jack Leigh, one of the top people at Gaumont.

All this I was to find out later, because my first job was not in the studio as such, but in the laboratory.

For a cameraman there is no better experience than to have worked in a lab. The normal practice in film-making is for the laboratory to assign a contact man to liaise with the cameraman. The cameraman will tell him beforehand that a particular scene is low-key, for example, or supposed to be taking place in moonlight. After viewing the rushes, he'll let the contact man know if they've been printed too light or too dark, or too red or yellow or blue, then the error can be corrected. If the cameraman has himself had lab experience, he's in a position to pinpoint any problem, and he can talk to the laboratory on equal terms.

When things go wrong they can go drastically wrong. There was once a film that was shot in Ireland, where the pillar-boxes are painted green. When the lab technicians saw the rushes they'd just printed, and noticed this green pillar-box, they panicked, thinking, oh my God, we've made a mess of this. So they did their damnedest to make it red. The best they could do was a shade of brown. Good communications between cameraman and lab would have avoided that.

When I was shooting *Lawrence of Arabia* in 1960 we travelled hundreds of miles to certain spots that David Lean liked because the sand of the desert was all red, or the rocks were white with streaks of black, or there was an interesting colour of mudflats. Left to their own devices, the lab people back in England might have reduced all these colour tones to an orthodox yellow.

In 1917 Gaumont had its own laboratory, so this kind of bad liaison didn't occur. Working there can best be described as like amateur still photography but on a grand scale.

The laboratory consisted of a series of interconnecting rooms, one for each stage of the process. First you did the negative, using red light for developing and yellow for printing. The negative-developing tank was made of teak and could accommodate up to three wooden frames, each holding 180 feet of film. You wound the film onto the frame until you came to a notch, which marked the end of the take, pinned each end of that section of film and placed it in the tank, shaking it gently to displace any air bubbles. After a few minutes you held it up and examined it by the red light. The image would gradually develop, and if you judged it wasn't ready you put it back in the chemicals for another moment or so. On average this would take five or six minutes. The next stage was the fixing tank, which contained hypo, for fifteen minutes, then the film was left for half an hour in a larger slate tank under running water. Finally it was taken into the drumming room, wound onto a large drum and left to dry. Later you carried out the same process to develop the print.

Nowadays each stage of processing is precisely timed, but in 1917 it was all a question of judgement. The same was true on the studio floor. There were no light meters then. The cameraman would look through the Debrie camera and see the image on the film, and think, I'll shoot this at f8. A bit later the sun would go behind a cloud – the studio was all glass, remember – and he'd open up the lens to f5.6. A good laboratory man could save the cameraman because if the film was shot under- or overexposed, allowance could be made in the developing.

The earliest light meters were like a watch with a roll of emulsion inside, which you held to the light. It would turn a shade of grey, and that would give you a rough idea. These were popular with still photographers but most cameramen preferred to rely on experience. Later, in the 1920s, more efficient light meters became available, and laboratory work became a more exact science.

We also had to mix our own chemicals. There was a forty-gallon tank, and you'd put in so many ounces of concentrated developer, adding warm water to make the required amount. To heat the water we had a huge cop-

A glimpse inside the production process at the Gaumont Studio, 1920. Freddie is at the far left of picture.

per geyser, about three feet high and over a foot wide. Every week I used to polish this till it shone. I would wash the walls, hose down the concrete floor and polish the floor in the office. I took a delight in keeping the place absolutely spick and span. It's important in a laboratory to have everything spotless otherwise you can get sparkle on the film. In the drumming room we had muslin over the windows to keep dust out. And when you wound the film onto the drum you'd rub the celluloid with a soft, damp, leather cloth to take off excess moisture – being careful not to touch the emulsion side and scratch it.

Another of my tasks was developing and printing the stills. These were taken on half-plate-glass slides on a wooden Sanderson camera with bellows. The slide was blown up in an enlarger to ten by twelve inches, the favourite size, or even bigger. The exposure might be two minutes, depending on the density of the negative. Sometimes I would first do a test, exposing a small piece of paper to see if I'd got the time correct. You could also make certain corrections. If the sky was rather blank I would try and produce a cloud effect by shading the lower part of the picture and giving the top more exposure. Or you could change the composition by using only a section of the picture and enlarging that.

When I'd been at Gaumont twelve months, the cameraman was called up and my boss, Harvey Harrison, went out on the studio floor to take his place. I was left in charge of the laboratory, completely on my own. This gave me the opportunity to experiment.

In those days various chemicals could be used to give the print a bit of colour. The unexposed (white) parts were tinted blue, say, for a night scene, yellow for sunshine, red for fire, and so on. Another series of chemicals affected the exposed areas, toning them sepia or copper, for example, as can be seen in old photographs. Before I started Gaumont weren't doing any of this. I read books on photography, wrote off for Kodak's formulae for tinting and toning, and added those chemicals to the laboratory stock.

First Men on the Moon, from the H. G. Wells story, was Gaumont's first big production at the end of the war. When I processed this I tried out a combination of tinting and toning. There was a dawn sequence which I tinted blue and toned pink, so that all the whites came out pink and the greys blue. The contrast of roseate sky against the bluish land was striking. In another sequence a character is in a workshop sharpening a piece of metal on an emery wheel, with sparks flying off. I used a fine camel-hair brush to touch up the sparks with yellow, red and amber dyes on two or three frames. These were little effects I would add to a print to be shown on a special occasion, such as a première.

After two years in the laboratory, first as assistant then as manager, I felt I had mastered the job. It was time to move on to something new. In 1919 the chance came. Gaumont closed its laboratory down, transferring all the processing to the works next door. I was sent to the studio to work as assistant cameraman.

2 Everybody's Assistant

The assistant cameraman, I learned, did all the jobs nobody else felt like doing. I took the stills, and developed, printed and glazed them. On location I drove the studio car, a 'Model T' Ford, and carried the camera. At the end of each day I projected the rushes. When the picture was finished, I cut the film. The director was supposed to do it, but in fact he just supervised, and I did the major part of the work, the same as an editor does today, although now it's more complicated because of sound. After the editing I cut the negative to match.

And of course I assisted the cameraman. The cameraman operated, while his assistant pulled focus. When necessary I would operate the second camera. The first thing I learned was how to turn it. At sixteen frames per second you made two turns every second. To keep to the exact beat you followed a rhythm in your head: one, tick, two, tick, three, tick, four, tick . . . It became second nature. Even now I can count the seconds of a minute pretty accurately. Sometimes you would turn the camera faster, for slow motion, or slower for a speeded up comedy chase sequence. The camera was on a tripod, with another couple of handles for panning. It was quite an art to be able to turn the camera and pan at the same time.

We worked all hours with no overtime, six days a week and often on Sundays too. Sometimes as a gesture they'd give us half a crown in the evening so you could go out and get some dinner. I didn't mind this at all. It was such a fascinating life I hardly noticed the time. Nowadays it would be impossible for a young man entering the industry to have this range of experience. Later on, the union insisted on one man, one job, but in the old days everyone used to muck in and do a bit of everything.

Anyone wanting to change this system had to contend with Colonel Bromhead, the managing director and, after 1922, owner of Gaumont. During the First World War he had been Director of Army Kinematography, and this showed in his style of management. One lunch-time there were a couple of chaps standing on a box in the studio yard urging us to form a union. Next day a notice appeared from Colonel

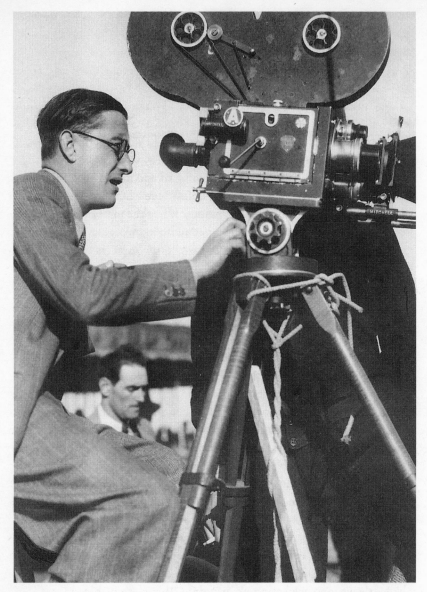

Skills of the silent cinema: Freddie operates the hand-cranked Mitchell camera.

Bromhead calling a meeting of all members of staff. At the appointed hour we assembled and presently the Colonel entered.

'Now I understand there was a meeting held in the yard yesterday,' he said. 'A union meeting, and you were addressed by two shop stewards. I should like these men to take two paces forward.'

The men in question stepped forth, and Bromhead said, 'Right, you're sacked. Go to the office and get your money.' Then he turned to the rest of us and said, 'Now, is anyone else interested in this . . . union? If so, please show yourselves.'

Nobody moved. So that was the end of that. After a long struggle the union was formed in 1933 and called the ACT (Association of Cinematograph Technicians). Incidents like this may explain why it tended to be bossy. 'An electrician is an electrician' became the rule; he wouldn't be allowed to pick up a prop. In later years if I were to grab a hammer and bang a nail in, the boys would laugh and joke because I was so bloody old, but just let anyone else try doing it.

I was willing to have a go in front of camera too. On *Saved from the Sea* (1922), directed by Bill Kellino, there was a scene in a quarry where an escaped convict leaps from a crane, landing (out of shot) on a blanket held taut by half a dozen people. The stunt man was the assistant cameraman: me.

Bill Kellino was one of Gaumont's top directors. From his circus background Bill brought a native wit and ingenuity, valuable qualities in that infant period of special effects. I was often assigned to him, and he became a kind of second father to me. He lived at East Sheen, just a mile or two from my present home, and I have vivid memories of spending weekends there, playing with his children in the garden. A couple of years later my eagerness to volunteer for anything could have cost me my life.

We were filming *Rob Roy* on location near Aberfoyle. High in the Trossachs a huge edifice of wood and plaster was built to represent Montrose's castle, besieged by Rob Roy's clan. On the day of shooting the battle we were expecting a man from Glasgow to do the stunts.

But this chap didn't show up. After a time I said to Bill, 'I'll do it, Mr Kellino. I'll do the fall.'

We climbed up the scaffolding and ladders at the back of the set, and looked down. At the bottom was a sheet with rope handles, held by sixteen men, four on each side, and underneath that a load of hay. From fifty feet up it looked like a pocket handkerchief.

Freddie takes a tumble from the crane on location in Cornwall for *Saved by the Sea* (1926).

Freddie (on horseback, centre) is enlisted for extra duties on location for *Rob Roy* (1922).

Bill said, 'No, no, it's much too dangerous.' I insisted, and finally he agreed. I dressed up as a MacGregor soldier, and we rehearsed the scene.

The cameras rolled. The Montrose soldier went for me with a dagger and I was sent flying over the battlements. I did a couple of somersaults in mid-air, felt something scrape against my tam-o'-shanter, and landed. Unhurt. I discovered I had come down right at the edge of the sheet, glancing the arm of one of the men *en route*. The director gave me ten shillings.

It was a big thrill to go on location, especially abroad. In 1926 I went to Paris on *Triumph of the Rat*, directed by Graham Cutts, one of the top directors of silent days, and starring Ivor Novello and Isabel Jeans. I remember climbing to the top of the Arc de Triomphe, lugging, as usual, the camera and tripod, a case of spare magazines over my shoulder. As I was setting off, the director thrust his script under my arm – just to add insult to injury. In one scene Ivor Novello was to dash across the Champs Elysées. Then they thought better of risking such a valuable property, so they dressed me up in the star's top hat and morning coat, and sent me out to dodge through the traffic.

Another interesting trip was to Egypt for *Fires of Fate*, an adaptation of Conan Doyle's *The Tragedy of the Korosko*, directed by Tom Terriss and starring two American stars, Wanda Hawley and Nigel Barrie.

The sea cruise, then the sight of Port Said under the pink dawn sky made a big impression on me, but the best thing of all was Tutankhamen. He was discovered during our visit, and we were among the first to see him. He was lying there, with his brown, shiny face, his whiskers, his gorgeous clothes, all in pristine condition. Around him were the gold objects – jewellery, cups, vases – that were found in his tomb. A few days later they noticed a deterioration had taken place as a result of his exposure to the air after thousands of years in an underground tomb, and he was put in a glass case. But we saw him in all his original splendour.

Between films I was sent to Denman Street, the headquarters of Gaumont Pictorials and the newsreel company Gaumont Graphic. I made several 'interest' films, short documentaries used as a filler in the cinema programme. One such was a film I shot on a cable-laying ship.

At Southampton I was greeted by the captain and shown to a beautifully appointed cabin complete with bottles of gin and whisky and a bowl of fruit. Fifty miles off The Lizard, where their instruments told them there was a break in the cable, the crew let down hooks. Both ends were brought abroad, welded together, and let go carefully so the cable didn't twist. All this time I was filming with my Debrie camera and one of its three lenses, from every conceivable angle including the crow's-nest. I made notes from what the officers told me, and the editor used these on the titles.

I did these jobs completely on my own. One had the same independence and flexibility as a reporter with his notebook. Apart from the Debrie, there were two other cameras suitable for newsreel work. The Eyemo was small and powered by clockwork, which made it handy in confined spaces. Several times I took it up in a plane and shot from the open cockpit, leaning out over the side. Holding only 100 feet of film (one minute), the Eyemo could be used only in short bursts. The other was the gyroscope camera, which had a 400-feet magazine. The principle behind it was that air pressure from a bicycle pump circulated through tubes inside, revolving a gyroscope. This kept the camera steady when you panned, so it could be hand held.

I covered the big sporting events, like the Grand National and the Cup Final. At the first Wembley Cup Final, in 1923, 150,000 spectators crammed in, spilling over onto the pitch. A newsreel film that has often been seen on TV shows a policeman on a white horse having a miraculously calming effect on the crowd. If that piece of film came from the Gaumont archives then I shot it.

I remember one Derby Day at Epsom. The organizers had set up a large packing case, about six feet off the ground, for me and my camera, and from there I filmed the crowds arriving, bookmakers signalling to one another, finally the race itself. I was stuck on my box and it started to rain. I only had a light raincoat, and soon I felt the raindrops trickling down the back of my neck. I thought, this is no good, I could catch my death of cold, so I sent a little boy to the refreshments tent to fetch me a drink. During the day I had a couple more. At the end of the week I presented my expenses book to the Gaumont accountant, Mr Stapleton, known as Sharky on account of his legendary strictness. He looked through it, and when he got to Derby Day, where I had written 'three double brandies to prevent double pneumonia', I saw his pencil stop. He fixed me with his gaze for what seemed like five minutes. I stared back. Then without any change in expression he signed it. I thought to myself, he's not such a bad chap. I was more than ready to stick up for my rights.

Fifteen years later this same Mr Stapleton worked at Alexander Korda's Denham studio. When Prudential Assurance, Korda's backers, realized how much money they were losing, they brought in Sharky to attempt some financial control. One of the first things he did was to replace toilet rolls with strips of newspaper. There he was, saving pennies while Korda frittered away thousands.

One of my newsreels was mentioned in the national press, under the headline 'Remarkable Endurance of Film Cameraman'. Two men on one-and-three-quarter-horsepower Francis Barnett motor bikes were attempting an ascent of Ben Nevis in the middle of winter. It was hell. There were blizzards, quagmires of mud, boulders all over the path. Four hundred feet from the summit, the snow came right up to their petrol tanks and they gave up. I thought, I'm not coming all this way without getting a shot from the top, so I carried on alone with my Eyemo. I dragged myself through waist-deep drifts to the summit, and got some beautiful shots at sunset.

Gaumont's great rival was Pathé News. The rights to photograph big occasions were bought by one of the newsreel companies, but then the chaps from the other organization would come in with cameras hidden under their coats or wrapped in parcels, and they'd take clandestine pictures. Each team would hire thugs to protect their own lot and harass the opposition. They would remove your film and expose it, giving you a roughing-up if you protested. I quite enjoyed these incidents.

This rivalry with Pathé extended to the sporting field. Gaumont had a sports ground for football, cricket, athletics, and so on. One day the assistant director Cyril Smith said to me, 'I want to put you down for boxing in the Charity Cup. What's your weight?'

'Me? I've never boxed in my life.'

'It doesn't matter,' he said. 'We'll get you a few lessons.'

He wouldn't take no for an answer, and they got an old pro named Pedlar Palmer to come down to the studio and teach me.

Came the fateful night we went down to the National Sporting Club. There was an exhibition bout by a current champion, a few other fights, then it was my turn. I was up against the man from Pathé for three three-minute rounds – which for a raw amateur is a hell of a long time. The first thing I discovered was this man was obviously a good boxer. Before I knew where I was he had hit me on the chin and I almost passed out. I pulled myself to my feet and went at him like a tiger. At the end I won on points and was presented with a silver cup. Outside I went straight to the toilet and was violently sick.

I was combative at football too. In a semi-final against a rough bunch of boys from the Harrow Mission, I was playing outside right. Every time I made a run down the wing their left back would trip me and I'd go sprawling in the mud. The third time he did it I lashed out, immediately getting a blow in return from one of his mates. The next minute all twenty-two players were fighting, and the referee stopped the match. A few weeks later we both appeared before the judges of the London Football Association in an old house in King's Cross. As we waited for our hearing I noticed the place seemed to be full of policemen. After being told I was disqualified, I found out why. Their offence was the same as mine: hooliganism on the field.

In 1918 the cameraman at Gaumont was Arthur Brown. He was followed by Billy Shenton, who despite having only one eye was considered pretty good. Another was Basil Emmott, the son of a wealthy man who owned the *Manchester Guardian*. Basil used to come down to the studio and hang around, observing, until they gave him a job as my assistant in the laboratory. He came up on the stage when I did, as second assistant cameraman. He bought himself a camera, a Pathé Willard, so if they needed a second camera they would use Basil. This camera fascinated me because I had until then only used the Debrie and the Eyemo. The handle was at the back instead of the side, and Basil had put chromium bits and pieces all over it. He was a great enthusiast, Basil. Later he worked at Warner's making quota quickies (cheap films made by American companies to comply with protectionist British legislation), where he gained the

The Gaumont football team, 1920. Freddie sits second from right of picture.
Beside him, front row centre, is team captain and Gaumont assistant director
Cyril Smith.

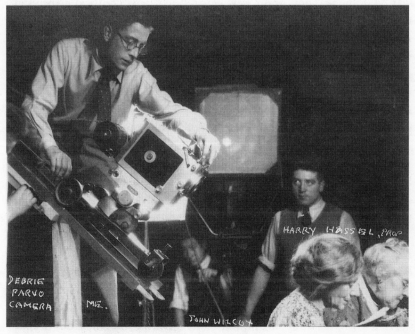

Freddie operates the Debrie Parvo camera, watched by prop man Harry Hassell.

nickname 'Burn 'em to a frazzle Basil', because he used so much light. Unfortunately, this association with trashy films ruined Basil's reputation, and in the last years of his life he got hardly any work.

Desmond Dickinson was an old friend of mine from this period. He was the cameraman at Stoll Studios in Cricklewood. I was once lent out to be an assistant cameraman there on a Scarlet Pimpernel film starring Nelson Keys. Four films were being shot simultaneously with four sets, four cameras, four crews, all in the same huge, long studio. It looked like a factory. Over the years Desmond and I often came across each other when we were lighting on adjoining stages in the same studio. Desmond was famous for eating cold potatoes. He told us it was his ambition that when he was too old to be a cameraman he would get a job as the doorman outside a studio. Then one day someone would ring the bell and there would be no answer, they'd look in the doorman's cubicle and find Desmond there, dead.

Most of the cameramen were older men who had come into the industry through God knows where. As a young man watching them I thought they were pretty crude. I would look at paintings by the masters and compare them with photography, and I began to think there must be a better way of doing it. There was a new generation that started about the same time as myself: Desmond, George Pearson's cameraman Percy Strong, and my great friend Bernard Knowles, who went on to film Hitchcock's *The Thirty-nine Steps*. We were getting better lamps and faster lenses and stock, so it was becoming possible to light a film with finesse. All I needed was the opportunity.

In 1927 I had been with Gaumont ten years and was earning £5 a week, which wasn't bad money, but I was still only an assistant. I'd had two screen credits – for *The Flag Lieutenant*, directed by Maurice Elvey, and *The Somme* – but only as second cameraman. One day the director of *The Somme*, M. A. Wetherell, said to me, 'I'm making a film soon for another studio. It's a big battle picture, set in the Great War, and I'd like you to be my cameraman.'

I went to see Colonel Bromhead to give him a week's notice. He was amazed. 'You're a fool, Freddie. This is the best company in England. We've got our eye on you. Stay with us and there'll be great possibilities for you here.'

'Yes, but I've got possibilities right now.'

He tried to dissuade me, pointing out the offer was for one film only and I would then be without a definite job. He promised me seven pounds ten shillings a week, which didn't cut much ice because Wetherell had offered twenty pounds. Finally we shook hands and he wished me the best of luck.

My break couldn't have come at a better moment. I was twenty-five years old, and planning to marry.

3 Lighting Cameraman

My wife was called Marjorie Gaffney, and she worked in films too. Starting off as a continuity girl, she became assistant director to Victor Saville, A. E. Dupont, Hitchcock and others. We went to live in Elm Park Mansions, Chelsea, in a fourth-floor flat with a fine view. I thought it was marvellous, being a newly married young man with the first home of our own. We were both very busy. I remember coming home after a day in the studio, and Marjorie was just leaving to do night work at Tilbury Docks on a film about the *Titanic*. Despite this, we found time to transform our flat. We made the walls white, got old bits of furniture and painted them black, and put up some blue chintz curtains. We were very proud of that flat.

By this time the members of my family had mostly gone their separate ways. Worn out from bringing up eight children on hardly any money, my mother had contracted tuberculosis. She spent six months in a sanatorium in Burgess Hill, Sussex, lying out on the balcony breathing fresh air, but then back in the smog of London her health rapidly deteriorated, and she died in 1920. Our father died not long afterwards. My three brothers had emigrated to Australia, and two of my sisters married. Soon after I married Marjorie the old family home was sold.

Victory was filmed in the autumn of 1927. Set in the last weeks of the Great War, the picture combined battle scenes with a spy story. A number of VCs took part, recreating their actual exploits, and the army gave us full facilities. We filmed trenches full of water, blasted trees, mud and fire and smoke. It was quite arduous, not to say dangerous.

In one scene we were filming a dugout, with a corrugated-iron roof, sandbags, a hole for the machine-gun, which was to be blown up. These things are notoriously difficult to control. I was photographing close, with my second cameraman, Joe Rosenthal, twenty yards back taking a longer shot. When the blast came, the roof of the dugout was sent flying straight towards me. I ducked, the corrugated iron went way over my head and landed on Joe, knocking him clean off his rostrum.

After a couple of months on Salisbury Plain the unit moved to Walton

Hall studio in Isleworth to complete the picture, and it was there I got my first real chance to do some lighting inside.

Sets and lighting at this time were primitive. The sets were canvas flats, similar to those used in the theatre. A stage-hand would drag a flat in and quickly fit it with a couple of braces at the back. There would be one practical door that opened, with others not used for the action simply painted in. The same went for the windows and the pictures on the wall. The sets were mostly two sides of a room. If the film was really ambitious you'd have three.

There were two kinds of arc lamp: the Winchester and the French-made Lebarden. The Winchester quartz was the same kind of lamp used for street lighting. Set in a glass bowl, it had two carbons, negative and positive, which crackled and fizzled, needed constant attention, and had to be replaced every day. It gave a bluish light suitable for the orthochromatic film then used, which was sensitive to blue. The Lebarden was a bank of carbon arcs with frosted glass in front, mounted on a tubular frame on wheels. The lamp itself was enormous, about three feet across, and it was the next best thing in strength to daylight. Neither of these arc lamps could be directed. Later on, Lebarden made a curved, dimpled mirror to put in front of the lamp so the light could be reflected. Around this time the first spotlights were introduced.

The way the older cameramen worked was first they'd get a long shot of the set, showing a character entering and walking over to a desk, say. Then they'd move in to a closer shot. To avoid the lighting being too symmetrical they might use a couple of arcs on one side, and three on the other. That was all. Otherwise the image was absolutely flat, just a flood of light. There was no attempt at artistry. There were some cameramen who used to keep a book, and they'd note down the lighting they'd used – how many arcs, how many feet away from the actors – so when they got to the next set they could refer to the book and do the same. You couldn't really call it lighting, it was just illumination.

As a cameraman I've always tried to make things look as they would in real life (with the exception of things like horror films or dream sequences, when you're trying for an expressionistic effect). For example, in a daytime scene I would arrange the lighting so it looks as if daylight is coming in through the window. Or if the shot includes a candle, I'd put a spotlight on the floor pointing upwards to hit the actor's face, with the room gradually going into darkness in the background; if the actor is near the wall I'd throw a shadow on that wall immediately behind.

On shore at Shoreham: cast and crew from *Daydreams* (1928), including Freddie (centre), Elsa Lanchester (to Freddie's immediate left) and Charles Laughton (far left of picture).

That was the kind of thing I tried to do even then, on *Victory*. It wasn't easy, given the limitations of the technology at that time, but still you can always do something if you have the will and the imagination.

After *Victory* I was offered various freelance assignments. Ivor Montague of Gainsborough Studio hired me to photograph three short films adapted from stories by H. G. Wells, whose son Frank was the art director there. Gainsborough – formerly the studio of Famous Players-Lasky, an American company – was in the middle of the slums of Islington. Hollywood stars would park their Rolls-Royces and come out later to find the emblem on the bonnet had been pinched. Our production was a modest affair; we had two or three little sets on the stage which we reused all the time, ringing the changes simply by redecorating and moving the furniture. Elsa Lanchester was in all three films, and one of them, *Bluebottles*, marked the début of her future husband, Charles Laughton.

Charles played a lecherous rajah who fancies a stage belly-dancer, played by Elsa. We'd have a close-up of Elsa's tummy and cut away to the rajah ogling her through his opera-glasses. After the performance she leaves the theatre only to be bundled into a car by the servants of the wicked rajah. Her true love, a French count (Harold Warrender), gives pursuit in a plane and corners the villain on his yacht. The rajah is thrown overboard to be snapped up by a passing shark, and the young lovers live happily ever after.

The real fun was doing the location off Southend, where for the shark's fin we used a piece of three-ply on a submerged float pulled along by a concealed line. Then it came to the drowning. Charles wasn't there, so Ivor Montague, who was roughly the same build, dressed up in the rajah's costume and jumped into the water.

'All right, Ivor,' I called out, 'the camera's turning.'

Ivor exhaled bravely and plunged his head under the water. However, we had reckoned without his natural buoyancy: his back disappeared but his large bottom remained afloat. After several seconds he came up spluttering, 'How was that?'

From the way we were falling about laughing he needn't have asked.

'You didn't sink, Ivor.'

'Oh. OK, let's try it again.'

The same thing happened again.

Ivor's assistant director was another generously proportioned man called Hankinson. Someone said, 'Let Hank try.' Hank put on the costume and did his best, but he too proved unsinkable.

I couldn't understand the problem because I'm one of those people who have to work hard when swimming just to stay afloat. 'It's the easiest thing in the world to sink,' I remarked.

'All right then,' Ivor said, 'you do it.'

My assistant operated the camera and I got in the water and breathed out and let myself go. I went down and down and down. I had my eyes open and the water was all green and when I came level with the keel of the yacht I thought, well, that's enough, and I started making strokes.

That's when it became difficult.

I didn't seem to be making much progress. The costume felt full of sandbags and my feet kept catching in the material. With no air at all in my lungs I started to panic. Just when I thought I was finished I broke surface and took a great gulp of air. I looked up and the crew were leaning over the side of the boat with worried expressions because they could see what a struggle I'd been having.

Fortunately we didn't need a second take.

While we were making these films I became friendly with Ivor who was a terribly nice, gentle sort of chap. He was a ping-pong champion and had visited the Soviet Union. To be frank I didn't then know what communism was, so I asked him, 'You're obviously an intelligent, well-educated man from a wealthy background. What made you a communist?'

'When I was a small boy, my father, Lord Swaythling, had a big house in the country. I was quite lonely and I made friends with the gardener's son and we used to play together. One day we went into the peach house and we both took a peach off the tree. We were in the middle of eating our peaches when in came the head gardener, and he slapped his son for stealing fruit and he sent him off crying. Then he turned to me and said, "I think you should go back to the house, sir." At that moment, Freddie, I was struck by the unfairness of things, and I've been a communist ever since.'

In the film world another kind of revolution was about to start. Over in the States a film called *The Jazz Singer* was breaking all records. The silent cinema had found its voice.

4 Booths and Blimps

The first two sound films made in Britain were *Blackmail* and *White Cargo*, and I had a hand in both of them.

The cameraman on *Blackmail* was Jack Cox, but Alfred Hitchcock asked me to do a montage – a short sequence of a dozen or so images each lasting two or three seconds – for the silent version. In later years each item would be shot separately, edited, then the whole sequence would be dissolved together in the lab during printing, but at this time all dissolves had to be done in the camera. It was a tricky business. Before you started you had to know the precise order of the images, and how many feet of film you wanted to use on each section of the montage. During filming it was often necessary to wind the film back or forward in the camera, and every time you did that you ran the risk of scratching it in the gate. If only one thing went wrong it would ruin the whole lot and you'd have to start all over again.

Hitch gave me a page of script, indicating – I forget the exact details – a shot of feet walking, followed by thunderclouds, a train, horses galloping. When I'd finished I showed it to him in the viewing room, and he said, 'That's fine, Freddie, but I've changed my mind. I'd like you to start with the train, then go to the feet and the horses' hooves, and finish with the clouds.'

So I had to go and repeat the process, which was his prerogative but annoying none the less. Many people have remarked that Hitch had a sadistic streak. On *Blackmail* there was a property man called Paddy, and he used to play all manner of tricks on him. He tested some handcuffs on Paddy, then 'lost' the key. While the search for the key continued, the prisoner was offered a cup of tea. The tea, Paddy soon discovered, contained laxative . . . Another time Hitch had Paddy bricked up in a chimney for a couple of hours. After these jokes he always slipped Paddy a pound.

Blackmail and *White Cargo* were originally made silent. A month or two later, when sound came in, the producers of both films decided to reshoot certain scenes with speech. The cameraman on *White Cargo*, Werner Brandes, had by then returned to Germany, and I was asked to take over the photography.

The studio was in a little house in the grounds of British International Pictures at Borehamwood. For soundproofing they padded the walls with blankets and draped felt under the corrugated-iron roof. Carbon arc lamps couldn't be used, because they spluttered noisily, and instead we had five-kilowatt and ten-kilowatt incandescent lamps. What with the extra-powerful lighting, the lack of ventilation and the insulation, it was unbearably hot, like being in a bakehouse.

We were given a week to complete this, because BIP wanted the studio back to do the sound sequences on *Blackmail*. We worked all Thursday and Friday nights – seventy-two hours non-stop – and finally got done early Saturday morning, shortly before the carpenters came in to pull down our set and construct the one for *Blackmail*. In between calls the actors lay down on the floor and napped as best they could in the sweltering heat. As the cameraman I couldn't do that, I was always needed. By the end I was walking about like a man in a dream.

Afterwards I drove the fourteen miles back to Chelsea in my little Austin seven with the assistant director, Arthur Barnes. I kept nodding off, hitting the kerb, waking with a start. Arthur said, 'Let's go and have a Turkish bath.' We went to a place in King's Cross. I can still clearly remember the steaming atmosphere, the massage, the shower, the hot towels – how delightful and fresh I felt. It seemed to take all the fatigue away.

White Cargo contains the first sound sequence to be filmed for a British feature, although *Blackmail* usually gets the credit for first talkie as it was released four months earlier, in June 1929, and because of Hitchcock's reputation.

By this time I was working for Herbert Wilcox. Herbert was one of the big successes of the post-war film industry. Starting out as a films salesman in 1919, he soon moved into production. Even from the beginning it was his policy to bring over the big names from Hollywood and the Continent, so that his films would sell overseas, and pictures starring Mae Marsh and Dorothy Gish – both D. W. Griffith protégées – were hugely popular. In February 1928 he and the actor Nelson Keys started their own company, British and Dominions Film Corporation, whose capital of half a million pounds made it one of the biggest in the industry. Later that year he asked me to join him as Chief Cameraman.

I think we only managed to make a couple of silent pictures. Herbert made a trip to Hollywood and, as he puts it in his autobiography, *Twenty-five Thousand Sunsets*, 'Yes, indeed! Talkies had come and were drawing the crowds. I cabled England to stop all silent production pending my return.' Herbert obtained land next to BIP, and the British and Dominions studio – soundproofed, air-conditioned, purpose-built and equipped with Western Electric sound – opened in 1930.

Sound was the asset, and it had to be used. At first, like most film companies in England and Hollywood, we concentrated on adaptations from the theatre. Herbert signed up big stars from the West End – the Yorkshire comedian Sydney Howard, song-and-dance man Jack Buchanan, the cast of the Aldwych farces. These farces were extremely popular. Starting with *Rookery Nook* in 1930, we filmed more than a dozen – *Plunder*, *Thark*, *On Approval*, etc. – all of them written by Ben Travers, starring Tom Walls, Ralph Lynn, Robertson Hare, Mary Brough, and directed first on the Aldwych stage by Tom Walls himself. Tom was a forceful man, rather domineering towards the rest of the cast, and mad about horses. In 1932 his horse, 'April the Fifth', was entered for the Derby and actually won. The whole studio had backed it, at twenty-five to one. When we went to collect our money, the bookie, standing to lose several thousand pounds, had run off. It was the only big win I've had in my life.

Photographing sound pictures required a new technique. The first problem was camera noise. Silent films had been shot at sixteen frames per second with a camera turned by hand. Now it was twenty-four f.p.s. – the increase was to accommodate the sound track – with a motor-driven camera, because for perfect sound synchronization the camera speed had to be exact. The cameras made a noise like a sewing machine, so they were put in soundproofed booths, big box arrangements like telephone kiosks on wheels. The operator was locked inside to film through a glass screen, and there he'd stay until the end of the take, when he'd stagger out sweating and gasping for air. These booths were so cumbersome it was impossible to do any but the simplest tracking shots.

After a year or two of using booths, blimps were developed. A blimp was a soundproof case that went round the motor and the operating parts of the camera. Lined with lead and rubber, these were very heavy – it took two men to lift one – but you could track more easily and go on a crane, so we got back some of the mobility we'd had in silent days. Nowadays soundproofing, made of the lightest materials, is built into the camera itself.

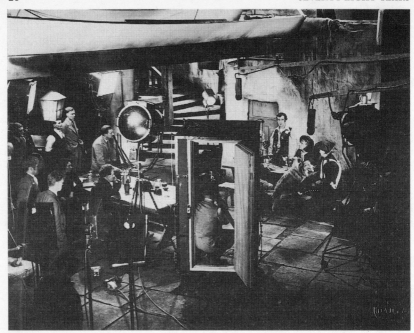

The cumbersome techniques of early talkies: Freddie in the soundbooth on *The Loves of Robbie Burns* (1931)...

... and working with the 'blimped' camera on location for *Mischief* (1931).

At the beginning of sound we used a system of multiple cameras. *Rookery Nook*, for example, had up to a dozen characters in a scene, with rapid interchange of dialogue. To film all this, with the necessary coverage of long, medium and closer shots, we had five cameras. These were ranged in a semicircle round the set, and each camera had four lenses on a turret so the operator could change lenses during the scene. The camera in the centre had a wide-angle lens to get the whole set as it would look to someone sitting in the front row of the stalls in a theatre. The next two cameras on each side took medium shots of various parts of the action, and the outside two did close-ups. There were no headphones but each operator had a detailed shooting script so that he knew on a certain dialogue cue he should be filming, say, a close-up of Tom Walls talking on the phone, while another camera was picking up a close-up of Ralph Lynn's reaction.

Preparation was elaborate but the actual shooting quite fast. We'd film a whole reel (ten minutes) at a time, one scene of the play. The actors had done it before on stage, so rehearsing was purely technical. And you lit once for the whole scene. Often we'd shoot a reel a day and finish the picture in a couple of weeks. Our record for an Aldwych farce was ten days. The editing was also simplified, because there was one soundtrack which ran for the whole reel, so the editor just cut the picture without having to worry about sound.

The technique has something in common with old-style TV drama. In both cases you have several cameras operating simultaneously, carefully choreographed to follow the action, which is continuous. With TV the cameras are highly manoeuvrable, the lighting effects more sophisticated, and the director can communicate with the operators by headphone, but there remains the same basic drawback: the lighting has to service the needs of all the cameras, so it's inevitably flat.

There still are occasions in film-making when it's better to use two or more cameras: for real events, like races and pop concerts, and for complicated action scenes that you only want to stage once, like fights, crowd scenes, car crashes. In 1983 on *Sword of the Valiant*, I used two cameras for certain scenes. Sean Connery had been hired for six days' work at a fee of one million dollars, so it was crucial to complete his scenes within that time. We had two cameras side by side, one getting a full-length figure, the other a waist shot, so we didn't have to film the scene twice from two different set-ups. From a lighting point of view it's not ideal working like that, but sometimes speed has to take precedence over perfectionism.

In silent days the cameraman lit and operated, and his one assistant did everything else. With sound and better lamps film-making became more sophisticated, and the camera team grew from two to four: the lighting cameraman, the camera operator, the focus puller and the clapper loader. The operator works the camera, assisted by the focus puller, who ensures each frame is in focus – often changing focus actually within the take. The clapper loader loads the camera, logs the film stock and works the clapperboard. As for the cameraman, he was eventually given the credit of Director of Photography, and this title gives a clearer picture of his actual task of lighting the set and planning the camera movements.

I'm often asked why the cameraman no longer works the camera. This is because during the take there is so much he needs to keep an eye on. In fact, he needs three eyes: one for the lighting – to watch out for a lamp flickering, an electrician forgetting to swing round a light, a shadow of some stage-hand appearing on the set; the second on the actors to see they keep to the arranged tempo and don't spoil the composition by unrehearsed movements; and the third follows the assistants on the camera to make sure they are doing exactly what they should.

Another new problem was the microphone. Eighteen inches long and shaped like a drainpipe, it would follow the actors round on a boom, with the sound man wanting it as close as possible to the speaker's head. Occasionally they would hide it in a vase of flowers or behind an ornament, but generally you'd have this damn mike floating about all over the place. I would say, 'You'll have to keep the mike up a bit. It's casting a shadow', and the sound man would retort, 'There's no point having pretty pictures if the audience can't hear what the fellow's saying.' Because sound was so new directors were rather bemused and tended to support the sound man.

Even today with directional microphones that can be turned to face the speaker and are not supposed to pick up extraneous noises, sound men are still quite fussy. On location, when there are car exhausts or planes passing overhead, they are always wanting to stop the scene. When I directed a film, in 1983, I was interested to find out during editing that many of the takes rejected by the sound man on account of background noise turned out to be perfectly all right.

When I worked for MGM at Elstree after the Second World War I made several trips to their Hollywood studio, Culver City. The situation there was even worse than at Elstree, with aeroplanes going over sometimes every half-minute. People who lived close to the studio hit on a novel way to supplement their income. When they saw a unit shooting on the lot they'd go out in their back yards and start practising the trumpet or using the lawnmower – anything just to make a noise – and the production manager would have to go over and tip them a few dollars to stop. In the end MGM made an edict that in no way was filming to be held up because of sound. If there was a problem the unit must shoot on regardless, and if necessary use post-synchronization. That came as a blessed relief. We got the same instructions at Elstree, so now we were able to snap our fingers at the sound men. Sound can always be added later but you can't do that with the photography. And you can double the cost of a film if you have hold-ups all the time.

The coming of sound changed film-making entirely. For the audience to hear words, natural sounds, music was a marvellous thing, of course. But it came at a price. Camera movement was less fluid, the lighting flatter. Actors tended to use their bodies less expressively. Stories were told in a more static way. The capital investment in sound equipment was astronomic, and film-making had to become an 'industry' – in the worst sense – to pay for it. Many people felt the romantic, buccaneering phase of the movies was over, the process had become a grind, the product a step backwards in terms of art. Generally speaking, I was not one of those. For me, photography with sound was an exciting challenge. But there were moments when I looked back.

One of our earliest sound films was *The Loves of Robbie Burns* (1931). The Scottish tenor Joseph Hislop as Burns sang 'Flow Gently, Sweet Afton', and Herbert wanted some scenic footage of the Highlands to cut into the song. My assistant Roy Kellino (son of Bill) and I set off for Scotland in a hired Daimler. We would be shooting silent with a hand-turned camera.

By the River Afton I put on a pair of waist-high waders. There were some big boulders just below the surface, and I clambered along these until I reached the middle of the fast-flowing stream. I planted the legs of the tripod in the bed of the river. I wanted the lens to be just above the surface, and it took me a while to get the camera steady, shortening one leg, lengthening the others. When I bent down to look through the lens, water poured into my waders, icy cold from the melted snow. I photographed two or three hundred feet of film, then I lifted the camera over my shoulder and struggled back to the bank, which wasn't easy with my waders full of gallons of freezing water. Roy pulled my waders off and I ran barefoot through stinging nettles and thistles back to the car. I remember having a piping hot bath, the landlord of the hotel bringing me

an extra-large whisky that made me instantly drunk, but most of all a terrific feeling of satisfaction at getting the shot.

In the finished film you see water rippling towards the camera and
mountains rising out of the haze in the distance. It's a lovely shot, and one
of my best last memories of silent filming.

5 Herbert and Anna

Herbert Wilcox, Anna Neagle and Freddie at British and Dominion in 1936.

This experimental period with sound lasted only a year or two. By the end of 1931 sound booths were out of date and we were once more using one camera. We had learned that when lighting is all-purpose – for three, or five cameras – it can't possibly be subtle. For the director too a single camera was preferable, so he could give his attention to getting the precise effect he wanted from each separate shot.

1931 was also the year when Herbert directed one of his biggest successes, a film that changed not only his life but also the pattern of our work together at British and Dominions for the rest of the decade. This was *Goodnight Vienna*.

Jack Buchanan, one of the big musical comedy stars in the 1930s, was in a West End show, *Stand Up and Sing*. Herbert was struck by one of the players, and decided to cast her as the leading lady in Jack's new film.

Goodnight Vienna made a star of Anna Neagle. She and Herbert fell in love, married, and made a string of hits together.

At first Anna was mainly a dancer. She had a sweet little voice but was not really a professional singer – in her early films her singing was dubbed by Anona Wyn. Under Herbert's direction Anna blossomed into an all-round entertainer and dramatic actress.

He chose her parts with care, casting her opposite accomplished leading men. He brought over Continental stars, such as the Italian Tullio Carminati for *The Three Maxims*, Belgian Fernand Gravet in *Bitter Sweet* and *The Queen's Affair* and Anton Walbrook, who played Prince Albert in *Victoria the Great* and *Sixty Glorious Years*. Her English co-stars included C. Aubrey Smith as Wellington, and Sir Cedric Hardwicke in *Nell Gwyn* and *Peg of Old Drury*.

I don't think Herbert was a great director in the sense of being a brilliant innovator and stylist like, say, Hitchcock. What he had was the popular artist's sure sense of his public, the flair for a good subject – seeing the appeal in stories about Nell Gwyn, Edith Cavell and Queen Victoria – and the ability to tell those stories with absolute conviction. He was also a good negotiator and promoter; he had a way with the Americans, getting many of his films distributed in the United States at a time when this was far from easy.

Britain in the 1930s was going through a terrible slump, but in the film industry it was a time of expansion: 33 features were made in 1926, by 1936 it was 192. British and Dominions films were doing very well at the box office, and I reckoned the fruits of my labour were there to be enjoyed. My first house was near the studio, at the foot of Deacon's Hill, between Elstree and Borehamwood, bought for the then enormous sum of £1,600; £500 down and the balance over twenty years – in fact I paid it off in three. In 1935 and 1936 Marjorie and I adopted two children, Barbara and Michael, and we moved to a five-acre farm, complete with stables, coach-house, orchard, and a full-time gardener – a lovely old chap who wore a green baize apron and gaiters. It seemed unbelievable for a kid from my background to have got this far.

At the time I was probably the highest-paid cameraman in Britain – not that I didn't earn it, working virtually fifty-two weeks a year. British and Dominions had three stages and we often had two or three films on the go at one time. At his peak Herbert was producing thirty films a year. I'd finish a film on 'A' stage with Herbert directing, and the following Monday morning start another one for Jack Raymond on stage 'B'.

When we needed a second cameraman Herbert would hire one for the duration of that particular film. On one occasion Jack Buchanan was to make his début as a director and Herbert had promised I would be available to do the photography. As Jack would also be acting it was doubly important to have a cameraman he could trust. After each take he'd ask, 'How was I, Freddie?', to which I might reply, 'Fine, but perhaps a bit over the top. You could tone it down just a little.' In a way I was co-directing. Anyway, the day we were supposed to start I was still tied up on Herbert's picture, which had overrun. Jack was worried. He didn't want to start without me.

Herbert could be very persuasive. 'I'm sure you can manage to do both . . .' For a week I photographed Herbert's film from nine to six, took an hour's break, then worked with Jack through till two in the morning.

For some people this kind of pressure can be a bit too much. Once we needed someone in a hurry and Herbert asked who I'd recommend. I asked Bobby Cullen, the production manager. Bobby said, 'What about Percy Strong?'

I wasn't so sure. In the 1920s Percy had been considered one of the best cameramen in the business, filming a string of Betty Balfour comedies for the highly rated director George Pearson. After leaving Pearson, Percy became an alcoholic and couldn't find work.

'No no,' Bobby insisted – he wasn't exactly a teetotaller himself, as a matter of fact. 'Percy's given it up. Doesn't touch a drop.'

So I was persuaded to recommend Percy to Herbert. On the first day of shooting, Percy went up to The Plough, a pub in Elstree popular with film crews, for lunch. Afterwards there was no sign of him. Jack Buchanan, the director, waited half an hour then came along to the stage where I was working and told me. I sent along my operator, Francis Carver, to take over. Around three Percy turned up, drunk and incapable. This happened a few more times and eventually he had to be replaced. After that I didn't see much of Percy. In 1940 we heard he'd committed suicide, jumping from a railway bridge into the path of an oncoming train.

It's a sad story, but in truth film-making is a ruthless business. When there's so much capital involved, and a day's delay can run into thousands of pounds, producers just can't afford to take a lenient view of human weakness. Redundancy is a common experience for film technicians, which is why the union made it so difficult for new people to enter the industry. When we changed from using five cameras to only one a lot of assistants suddenly found themselves out of work. Losing one's job can, however, have its lighter side. Take the story of Ivan Foxwell . . .

There's an old saying in the film business: 'Always be kind to your assistants because in a few years they might be your bosses.' We were going through a thin time, and Herbert said, 'I'm afraid I'm going to have to lay some people off. How about Ivan Foxwell?' Ivan was a clapper loader. He also happened to be the son of someone well known in the City. Herbert liked to invite VIPs to the studio. He'd show them round and they'd come across Ivan and say, 'Hello, Ivan. Fancy seeing you here. How are you?' I don't think Herbert liked that at all, seeing his important visitors making such a fuss of his humble clapper loader. Not that this was a reason for sacking him. As the numbers boy, the lowliest member of the camera team, Ivan was the most expendable.

'Ivan's a bright lad, and he's doing very well,' I told Herbert. 'If possible, I'd like to keep him on.' Herbert relented, but a few days later the subject came up again. Finally I said to Ivan, 'Sorry, but I'll have to give you a week's notice.' He understood I'd done my best for him, and there was a sad farewell and he left.

A few weeks later Ivan was back. Through his wealthy friends he managed to scrape some money together to set himself up as a producer, and now he wanted to rent some of Herbert's studio space. In the event he decided our studio was too expensive. Later Ivan became a successful producer, making, amongst other pictures, *The Colditz Story*.

I had about a dozen assistant cameramen. As Chief Cameraman, both at British and Dominions and later at MGM, I always tried to make sure they had a good apprenticeship. Many of them went on to become directors of photography or directors. Among them were Freddie Francis, Jack Cardiff and (of a later generation) Nicolas Roeg, and I've often been told, 'I've learned a lot from you. You gave me a bloody good training.' In a sense it was much easier in those days for young cameramen working for a big company. You might be photographing a comedy one week, a love story the next, whatever it happened to be. You were just assigned to the next picture. With the collapse of the studio system it has become more difficult for young cameramen to get this range of experience. I don't think cameramen these days are as well trained as they used to be.

I tried to give my assistants a break whenever I could. One time Jack Raymond needed a cameraman and I asked Bernard Knowles's younger brother Cyril, who'd been a successful operator for a number of years, if he would like to do it.

'Oh, no,' he protested, 'I don't think I could. I'm not ready for the responsibility.'

Cast and crew of *Calling Bulldog Drummond* (1951). Freddie sits on the floor.
Beside him with clapper is his assistant at the time, the young Nicolas Roeg.

'I think you're bloody silly,' I told him. The opportunity was there and
he didn't grasp it, so I offered it to another assistant, Cyril Bristow, who
jumped at it. In the film business you don't always get a second bite at the
apple.

We were a happy team at British and Dominions. Herbert was always
on the lookout for talented collaborators. Having hired someone –
wisely, generally – he'd leave him to get on with his job without interfer-
ence. At the beginning of sound he brought over some American experts
to help us through the early technical problems. When the sound man,
Duncan Mansfield, arrived, we found he was practically stone deaf,
although this didn't seem to stop him being good at his job. Byron 'Bun'
Haskin, originally a cameraman, later a science-fiction director, was an
experienced all-round technical man and another useful asset to us.

Twenty years later I photographed Walt Disney's *Treasure Island* for
Bun. He managed something that proved too difficult for many other
directors: he tamed Robert Newton. At the beginning Bun, who liked a
drink himself, said to Newton, 'Look, Bob, I'll make a pact with you. If
you stick to ginger ale, I'll do the same. We'll both go on the wagon for the
picture. How about it?' Newton agreed. And he did manage to abstain
during the filming. The night we finished there was an almighty booze-up.

Our editor was a brilliant American, Merrill White. David Lean, who was for a time an assistant editor at British and Dominions, later told me Merrill taught him everything he knew about editing. Later on Merrill became known as 'The Doctor', because he would be asked to save a botched film, adding a few inserts and twisting things round to make it effective.

The fashionable designer Doris Zinkeisen also did some work for us – partly for snob value, I suspect. Her sexy dress for Anna Neagle in *The Little Damozel* got a lot of attention, but some of her contributions were less successful. The transparent Perspex bed she designed for *Carnival* was so unsound our art director had to reinforce the legs and support it with overhead wires before anyone could sit on it. As Laurence Olivier puts it in his autobiography, a designer is someone who scribbles a drawing on the back of an envelope which the art director then has to make function.

Our art director was L. P. Williams, known as 'Bill', a colleague for ten years who became a close friend. One of the perks of our jobs was to recce locations together. I remember the Alps in 1935 and getting up at the crack of dawn to climb halfway up the Matterhorn to take a look at a lake near the snowline. The lake turned out to be rather black and uninterest-ing, not exotic at all, and my stills camera started to weigh a ton. Coming down we kept our spirits up by planning in great detail what we'd have for breakfast – bacon, kidneys, how many eggs . . . In Merano in Italy we hired a Hispania Suiza car with white curtain awnings, and explored Lake Garda, which proved to be the perfect romantic setting we were looking for.

Bill was somewhat military in his bearing – with a moustache to go with it – and I remember him tearing a strip off a Venetian barman who served us brandy with ice. During the war he served in the camouflage unit in Egypt, making mock-up tanks to mislead the enemy, and after-wards he was chief art director at Pinewood on a white elephant of a scheme called Independent Frame. This was intended to solve the prob-lem of the uncertain English weather. Some bright spark had the idea of shooting all exteriors in the summer, then in the winter they'd go into the studio and use this footage as background. It was all very well organized with white lines painted on the stage like a draughtboard to help them line up the shot against the back projection. They even had a unit of weather forecasters at Pinewood who reckoned they were right 50 per cent of the time – which meant they were wrong 50 per cent of the time. It ended up as an expensive failure for the simple reason that English weather in the summer is almost as bad as it is at other times of the year.

In 1983 Bill Williams and I attended a special screening of *Victoria the Great*, restored in a new print for the National Film Archive. Seeing the film after forty-six years, I was quite impressed. It didn't seem particularly dated. I pride myself that British and Dominions were just about the tops in British film-making in those days, turning out class films. I remember the first crane we had, knocked together in our workshop from bits of angle-iron with counterweights at the back. By 1937 our equipment was much more sophisticated. We had a dolly with big balloon tyres, made narrow so it would pass through doors and fit easily on a truck for going on location. We named it the Wilcox dolly, and it was widely used in the industry for some years.

Freddie with Anton Walbrook, Anna Neagle and Herbert Wilcox, on location for *Victoria the Great* (1937).

In the last reel *Victoria the Great* bursts into colour – making it the first British feature to include a colour sequence. Technicolor sent over a cameraman called Bill Skall to advise me on the lighting and the use of the cameras, which used three negatives and were heavy and cumbersome. As well as Bill, who was friendly and helpful, I had to put up with Natalie Kalmas, wife of the inventor of Technicolor, whose title on the film was 'Technicolor Director'. She came on the set about twice, delivered a few disparaging remarks like 'I don't like that shade of blue' – but since she was judging it without the correct lighting we weren't very impressed with her.

King George VI liked *Victoria the Great*, and Herbert seized the opportunity of asking for location facilities for its sequel, *Sixty Glorious Years*. We were given Balmoral, Windsor Castle, Osborne House – the lot. The Queen and Princess Margaret have both since told me they recall watching us from a window in Buckingham Palace filming in the court-yard below.

Herbert was quite a thrifty film-maker – unlike his rival Alexander Korda whose extravagance almost bankrupted the industry – and his films looked more expensive than they were. *Victoria the Great* was made in five weeks on a budget of only £150,000. He was a shrewd entrepreneur but in some ways he was unrealistic. On many occasions he'd come in on a Friday morning as usual and we'd discuss the scene. Leaving me to line up the shot, he'd nip up to town to raise more money. He needed to do that simply to pay the wages. By four he'd be back, mission completed, we'd shoot the scene and finish about six. He'd say, 'Fine. Three minutes' footage. That's a good day's work.'

It wasn't that he ran over schedule, but he was an eternal optimist – he didn't have enough money to start with. He'd tell his backers it was a four-week schedule, and he would finish in four weeks, or think he had, then later Merrill White, the editor, would say, 'Herbert, I need an insert for the ballroom scene', and we'd return to the stage and do some more filming. In a way he was pulling the wool over the eyes of his backers by saying he had finished. Up to 1936 he could afford to cheat a bit because we still had our studio.

I say 'had' because in that year there was a disaster. It happened over a weekend when Marjorie and I were staying in a hotel in Brighton. In the middle of the night I was awoken by a phone call from two of my assis-tants, Skeets Kelly and Jack Cardiff. The studio was on fire.

'What about the cameras?' I asked.

We had two Mitchells, bought second hand from Hollywood, and two little old cameras, an Eyemo and a Vinton. One of the Mitchells used to give us a lot of trouble – scratching the film and being unsteady – and was constantly being patched up in the workshop; we called it 'B' Mitchell.

'It's all right,' they said. 'We managed to save the camera equipment.'

'You should have left that bloody old Mitchell,' I said, thinking of the insurance money. I'm afraid that's all the thanks they got from me.

On the Monday morning I went down to the studio, which was still smouldering and completely gutted. The fire was caused by an electrical fault in the roof. We had been due to start a new picture, *London Melody*, that very day. A week later it became the first film to be shot at Pinewood, then a brand-new studio. From then on our films were made either at Pinewood or, as with *Victoria the Great*, at Denham.

When it came to filming *Victoria*, Herbert fell out with his business partner, C. M. Woolf, the distributor, who didn't think the subject suitable for Anna. Undeterred, Herbert went ahead on his own, putting in all his savings (at the end of his career he was to do this once too often and lose everything), with distribution from RKO. This link with RKO prospered, and in 1939 they asked Herbert to film *Nurse Edith Cavell* in their studio in Hollywood. I was to go with him as his Director of Photography.

6 'A' Picture or 'B' Picture?

'But Herbert,' I protested, 'they'll never let me work there.'

'Why ever not?'

'British technicians are never allowed to work in Hollywood. It's a closed shop. The unions won't stand for it.'

'Oh, don't worry. We'll soon fix that.'

And on that note we set off. We sailed across the Atlantic on the *Aquitania*, Herbert and Anna, Bill Williams, myself and two Americans, Merrill White and his young assistant Elmo Williams. In New York Elmo told me he was going to buy a car and drive to the west coast. Would I like to accompany him? 'We'll take it easy,' he said. 'Five hundred miles a day, and we'll stay in motels wherever we happen to end up. We should do it in nine days.'

The car was an Oldsmobile with fans and heaters and all those other things we didn't have back home. We'd travel for hours through hot deserts with the windows wide open and the fan on, then climb to some high spot where it was freezing cold. As an Englishman I wasn't used to such extremes of climate. One very hot day the fan belt broke and we ground to a halt amidst the flies and the suffocating heat. Elmo managed to fix it with a piece of wire, and we limped into the next town at ten miles an hour.

In Arizona we reached the top of a pass and stopped to admire the spectacular view. At a little shelter where you could buy a cup of coffee we chatted to the owners, an elderly man and his wife and daughter.

'I'm a New Yorker,' he said. 'I was in business, doing pretty well for myself. Then the crash came and wiped me out. All we had left was the car and a few hundred dollars. So we thought, what the heck, let's go to California. By and by we reached this spot, and we camped here for the night. Next day we got up and it was so beautiful we decided to stick around another night. Some farmers came by and left us a chunk of meat and a sack of potatoes. That was a year ago. We set up this little coffee place and we've been here ever since. It's the happiest time of my whole damn life.'

But Elmo and I had to press on. We visited Grand Canyon and Boulder Dam and finally arrived at Hollywood.

Then came the moment of truth when the union said no way would they allow me to work. Herbert went to the management of RKO, and he argued with the union. This was his first film in Hollywood, he pointed out. The technicians and work practices would be unfamiliar to him, and to Anna, whereas I had been photographing her for eight years. In the end it was agreed I could do it, provided there was an ASC (American Society of Cinematographers) cameraman standing by on full salary.

I only had a visitor's permit, which meant I had to leave the country and re-enter on a labour permit. Merrill White drove me the 250 miles to the nearest border, a town called Calexico in the USA and Mexicali on the other side. He sat waiting in the car while I went through immigration. 'You do realize', the officer informed me, 'that when you go out into Mexico, you won't necessarily be allowed back?'

'I'll take that chance.'

I went through both borders, walked a few hundred yards up the white dusty road, then returned. I passed quickly through the Mexican post, and approached the United States.

The immigration officer examined my passport, then ushered me into a ridiculously small room where about thirty Mexicans sat dozing in the stifling heat. In my memory I stayed there about twelve hours, though I suppose it must have been less, but long enough anyway to dwell on the horror stories I had heard about people being detained in such places for weeks on end. Then they took me to another room, where I was stripped and examined by a doctor. For some reason he paid particular attention to my eyes, peering into them, and the skin of my chest and arms, which he squeezed and prodded.

'OK, get your clothes on,' the immigration officer said. 'We had to make sure. You see, a while back a murderer escaped across the border. Fella about your age and height. An Englishman, as a matter of fact. And his name was Frederick Young.'

'Is that so?'

'Yeah. But he had blue eyes and a number of tattoos. We had to check you out for any sign of skin grafts and to see if you were wearing contact lenses. You're clean, Mr Young. Welcome to the United States.'

Next day at the studio there was a production meeting – something unknown in England – with about twenty people, including various chiefs of department, and at the head this tough production manager.

'OK, Mr Wilcox, let's get the ball rolling. I wanna know, is this an "A" picture or a "B" picture?'

This was a new one on us. 'I don't know,' Herbert said. 'What's the difference between an "A" picture and a "B" picture?'

'If it's an "A" picture, the sky's the limit, but then if it flops, you're out. With a "B" picture you have a reduced schedule and if it's a success, you're in, you're a hero.'

'In that case,' Herbert declared, 'it's a "B" picture.'

'Right, I'm going to reduce your schedule to six weeks and cut your budget for sets in half.'

A couple of days later we went on the stage to start shooting. The first set was a cell where Nurse Cavell was in prison, charged with spying. I was introduced to the gaffer, a big, thickset guy.

'Good morning, Mr Young. All right, boys, light 'em up!'

On went all these lights to give a brightly illumined set. He seemed to have hit a lamp on each wall. It would have photographed acceptably, but it was just bright light with no atmosphere. Normally the cameraman goes on set and considers what is required – the time of day, the artificial light in the room, the kind of mood – and sets about lighting accordingly. I was a bit nonplussed to find the gaffer had done it for me. I thought for a moment, then said, 'All right, Hank, kill 'em and we'll start lighting it.'

'What's the matter? Don't you like what I've done?'

'Well, no doubt it's very good,' I said, trying to be diplomatic, 'but you know, this is supposed to be a dawn sequence.'

He was somewhat disgruntled, but after a few days it was smoothed over and we got friendly with everyone and the crew accepted me as one of them. Later I got to know other Hollywood cameramen and they explained that it was not unusual for the gaffer to pre-light the set. Producers liked it because they thought it speeded things up. Gaffers liked it because it gave them a sense of importance. And as for the cameraman, if he was weak or lazy he put up with the practice. 'Your reputation will suffer if you allow it,' I was warned, 'because you'll be associated with inferior work. Never let a gaffer light your set, because then you're a dead duck.'

My American crew was very good. The operator was a chap of about forty who always had a cigar in his mouth. At the end of the take I'd ask, 'How was it?' and he'd growl, 'OK.' He never asked for a second take. Often an operator will be over-perfectionist and say, 'I'm not quite happy about it. I'd like another go', so you carry on, but the actors are tired and

more likely to fluff, and you end up doing seven or eight takes. Afterwards
I cited this American to my operators back home as an example of someone who gets it right first time.

The scope and efficiency of Hollywood studios impressed us. Bill
Williams and I visited all the studio lots, arranging to use a French street
at one and a tank for canal scenes at another. There were complete sets for
small towns, railway stations, docks, airports, etc., covering in total hundreds of acres. The companies rented each others' sets, thus saving enor-
mously on production costs. In the southern California sunshine these
sets stood for years, needing only the occasional coat of paint.

The climate allowed films to be made the year round, so department
heads were able to build up good teams and keep them working together.
This showed in their special effects, which were way ahead of ours. On
Nurse Edith Cavell I remember a couple of men darting around with little machines of a kind I'd never seen before, making a lovely mist. They
also had much better lamps and cameras.

Ensconced at RKO in Hollywood: Freddie observes Anna Neagle at work in
the title role of *Nurse Edith Cavell* (1939).

Freddie larks with the great Lee Garmes, famed collaborator of Sternberg, at Garmes' beach house in Laguna.

It was a gruelling six-week schedule, with Bill required to turn out eighty sets with little time for preparation, but we managed to finish on time. *Nurse Edith Cavell* was voted 'Best Picture of the Month', whatever that meant.

The cameramen in Hollywood gave me a warm welcome. Lee Garmes, best known for his films with von Sternberg and Marlene Dietrich, such as *Shanghai Express*, invited me down to his beach house at Laguna. I remember waking up on the Sunday morning to the sun streaming through the blinds and the roar of the sea on the rocks a few yards away. It seemed an idyllic lifestyle. Another time Lee and his wife took me to their ranch. These Hollywood cameramen, who enjoyed a standard of living quite unknown in England, all had a second string to their fiddle. Lee's line was avocados. Joe August had a concession on some place in the desert where there was a white rock dust he had packaged and sold as face make-up.

I met Charlie Rosher, Mary Pickford's cameraman, Joe Ruttenberg, whom I corresponded with for years until his death in 1983, and Gregg Toland, who later photographed one of my favourite films, *The Grapes of Wrath*. It was around this time that he and Orson Welles were making *Citizen Kane*, also at RKO.

In *Citizen Kane* they decided to film with deep focus, which was then regarded as something new. In fact there's nothing new under the sun: things are discarded, then come back. There always has been deep focus, although admittedly in the early days it was less easy to achieve because the film stock was slower. To get deep focus you stop down the iris of the lens; instead of the normal 2.8 or 3.5 you shoot at f16, and to compensate for the smallness of the aperture you need a lot of light.

Over the years I've often been asked to do deep focus, generally by directors who've seen *Citizen Kane* and want to copy it. I say, 'OK, but you realize it means using a hell of a lot of light. The set'll get very hot and the actors will fry. If we're on location filming in a real house it'll be even worse because there'll be no air-conditioning and we won't be able to have the windows open because of noise from the street outside. It'll be pretty unpleasant, and everyone's going to get bad-tempered.' The usual reply is, 'Ah, yes, I see what you mean. Well, we'll see how it goes', and that's the end of the matter.

The main objection to deep focus is not practical but aesthetic. The eye automatically focuses on the sharpest point of the screen. If the background has equal definition, the audience's attention will wander from the action in the foreground to the décor behind. There may be a compelling reason to do this; for instance, you want to show someone in the background spying on someone in the foreground. (An interesting challenge for the cameraman, because technically you need a lot of light while for dramatic reasons you might want it to be a semi-dark room.) In the old days it was common to put a gauze round the lens – often a ladies' stocking with a hole in the middle burnt by a cigarette – so that only the face was in focus surrounded by a fuzzy halo. This now looks artificial, but the general principle of making the audience concentrate on the character in the foreground still holds.

After *Nurse Edith Cavell* Herbert asked me to do another picture with him in Hollywood, but the war was about to start and I wanted to get back to my family. I could have stayed, and if so I might still be there today, but I felt I could never be happy living anywhere but England. Besides, there were grave problems with my health – or so I believed.

It started near the end of the picture. On set there was always a nurse in a smart uniform. One day she remarked, 'You're not looking very well.'

'Yes, I am feeling a bit groggy,' I admitted. 'I think I've got a touch of 'flu.'

She took my pulse. 'I don't want to alarm you, but I think you should see a doctor.'

I was referred to a heart specialist, who told me I had a heart block. 'You must follow a strict diet,' he told me. 'And I'll give you two kinds of pills – one to make your heart beat faster, the other to slow it down. Feel your pulse every hour. If it's above a hundred take the blue pill, less than forty-five the red one. All right?'

I emerged from the consultation sixty-five dollars poorer but relieved to be alive. From that moment on I was convinced I was at death's door. Marjorie had joined me and we took a trip to San Francisco to the World's Fair. I had some students push me round in a wheelchair like an old man.

Back home I immediately rang my GP to tell him the bad news. A few minutes later he phoned back. 'I've made an appointment for you with Sir Maurice Cassidy, the King's heart specialist –'

'Oh, good.'

'– on Thursday.'

'Thursday? I want an appointment tomorrow. I might be dead by Thursday.'

He told me Sir Maurice was a busy man, so I resigned myself to the delay, and the following Thursday turned up at Harley Street. We went through the same routine as in Hollywood – ECG, X-ray, various other tests – then Sir Maurice said, 'My dear fellow, there's absolutely nothing wrong with you.'

'But I was told to take it easy going upstairs.'

'Run up and down the stairs. Do you good.'

'What about the diet?'

'Chuck it away.'

As we were talking I felt myself suddenly feeling much better.

'My advice is, take your family and have a nice holiday by the sea.'

We went to Gara Rock, near Salcombe in Devon, and stayed at a hotel perched on a cliff top with a steep path down to the beach. All day I was swimming and climbing on the rocks and playing with our two children, aged four and three. Then I'd give one of them a piggyback, charging up the cliff path for lunch. I felt as fit as a flea, and I remembered Sir Maurice's opinion of his colleague in Hollywood: 'He's a bloody fool.'

7 Propaganda and Patriotism

I got back to England just as the war was starting. My contract with Herbert Wilcox had expired, and my first thought was to join the services, but my age was against me. It seemed ironic: too young for the first war, too old for the second. Instead I photographed a war film for Michael Powell.

49th Parallel was the first film to be commissioned by the Ministry of Information, and it had an explicit propaganda purpose. In the story a German submarine enters Hudson Bay, where it's bombed by the Canadian Air Force. The sailors stranded on shore have no means of escape, so they head for the American border. The idea behind the film was to suggest Nazi Germany posed a threat to the United States, and persuade the American audience that the US should abandon its neutral status and join in the Allied war effort.

A real U-boat almost scotched the project – not to mention our lives – before we even got started. We left Southampton on the *Duchess of Richmond* at full speed at dusk, accompanied by another liner and a destroyer. Next morning we awoke to find ourselves alone on the ocean. The destroyer had turned back for further escort duty, and the *Andorra Star*, with its complement of several hundred Italian prisoners-of-war, was torpedoed and sunk with all lives lost.

Michael Powell was something of a martinet, and it wasn't long before he was called on to crush a little dissension in the ranks. I was sitting opposite him at dinner one night when I noticed Finlay Currie engaged in a vehement discussion with another actor, John Chandos. Suddenly Finlay, who was the oldest member of the cast and had a glass eye, reached over and struck John. I said to Mickey, 'Don't look now, but Finlay's just punched John Chandos.'

Powell jumped to his feet and ordered the whole unit to his cabin. Casting us a stern look, he said, 'Get this straight. I want you to realize there's a war on. We are on a special mission to make a propaganda film. And we're the only men on a ship full of women and children. So I don't want any misbehaviour. Now, what's this about? I understand, Finlay, you hit John?'

'Yes, I did,' came the defiant reply. 'Chandos said something derogatory about the King. So I punched him on the jaw. And if he repeats it I'll do it again.'

In the film Finlay plays the part of the Hudson Bay factor and Chandos is one of the Nazis who terrorize him.

We spent four months in Canada, travelling 20,000 miles from Baffin Island in the north to Niagara Falls and west as far as Banff in the Rockies. Canadian Pacific transported us free, but some locations were so remote they could only be reached on horseback or foot. Powell was a keep-fit fanatic. He used to pride himself on leaping up those mountains. He had special boots with spikes and we'd see him disappearing into the distance while we toiled after him lugging the camera. When we got there he'd be further up on the next rise. Finally I shouted at him, 'For Christ's sake, come down and shoot from here. It's just as good.' He just stood there, arms crossed, legs apart, glaring at me. I didn't move. On a long, arduous location the atmosphere can get a bit taut now and then.

In one scene the Nazis' stolen aeroplane runs out of petrol and crash lands in a lake. For the tail part of the plane we used a replica. The actors had to struggle out of this dummy and swim to the shore, while we filmed them from two angles. I was on the shore operating the main camera, while Skeets Kelly took a closer shot with the Newman-Sinclair from a raft supported on oil drums. When everyone was ready Michael Powell gave the word.

Niall MacGinnis, playing a Nazi, was the first out, followed by Raymond Lovell. Raymond wasn't a natural swimmer, and he was soon in trouble. Niall turned back to help him, and Skeets dived in too. As he did so, the raft tipped over and the Newman-Sinclair fell into the water. Skeets, like a true professional, plunged down after our precious camera.

Everybody joined in, trying to help poor Raymond. When he was two or three yards out, I went in and pulled him ashore. Water was pouring out of his mouth and he looked half dead. Someone started pumping his chest to revive him. In the middle of the crisis Mickey Powell strolled along, a supercilious smile on his face, and remarked, 'Oh, come on, fellas, don't let's make too much of a fuss.'

Eric Portman turned on Mickey, his voice shaking with rage. 'You callous bastard. The man's nearly dying and that's all you can say?'

Raymond recovered, unlike the character he was playing who actually does die at that point. A few days later the rushes were screened, in front of the whole unit. The camera that I'd been operating from the shore had been left running, and everything was there – the struggle in the water, the uproar and confusion as Raymond is dragged ashore, then Eric Portman laying into Michael. We all sat po-faced listening to this. Michael didn't turn a hair and no one said a word.

As for the camera, Skeets managed to save it, and when stripped it was found to be all right. The magazine was evidently a tight fit, and some of his footage was used in the finished film.

Filming in such remote places meant we could take no generators, only reflectors. For a night shot in a tepee we improvised the lighting by using flares. An ordinary blimp would have been too heavy to carry around, and on the boat to Baffin Island I made one out of lightweight local materials – cotton waste and caribou hide. After this my sewing skills were much in demand making watch-straps and leather mittens for others in the unit.

Our salaries were paid in England and we were given a small allowance, sufficient for a bottle of beer and some cigarettes, by the production manager, George Brown – 'Dollar-a-Day Brown', as we called him. During the voyage across Hudson Bay a plot was hatched to get at the bottle of brandy George kept for emergencies. The make-up people painted my face a deathly white with a bit of green under the eyes. Hearing I was ill, George came rushing in. He took one look at my face, ghastly under the naked bulb of the reading light over my bunk, and cried, 'Oh my God, what can we do?'

'Give him some brandy, you idiot,' somebody called out.

George fetched the brandy, and when he got close I grabbed it and took a swig. He enjoyed the joke. Later I found a more effective means of extortion. I had brought my Eyemo, which proved handy because unlike the other camera it could be used without a tripod. Mickey Powell was constantly asking to borrow it. I said to George and Mickey, 'I'd like some money for the hire of the Eyemo.'

'Sorry,' replied George, 'I'm afraid that's not possible.'

'In that case, it's not available any more.'

'Pay him,' Mickey snapped. He didn't even look round. With the pound a day rental I was able to buy the boys extra bottles of beer.

The Nazis in the story encounter various plucky individuals who in standing up to them deliver the film's anti-Fascist message (scripted by Powell's long-time associate Emeric Pressburger, who won an Oscar). These parts were played by Laurence Olivier (as a French-Canadian trapper), Leslie Howard and Anton Walbrook, none of whom accompanied us on location. One star who did was Elisabeth Bergner.

49th Parallel: Freddie at work with Glynis Johns, Laurence Olivier and Michael Powell . . .

. . . and on the Denham 'outdoor' set. The actors before the camera are Leslie Howard, Eric Portman and John Chandos.

As an Austrian citizen, Elisabeth needed special permission to go to Canada, granted on the proviso she returned to complete the film at Denham. The character she played was a Hutterite. The Hutterites were a strict rural community of Lutherans. After marriage the men never shaved, and the women all wore simple black dresses with white spots and were forbidden any adornment such as make-up. The community produced all their own food and clothing, and were dependent on the outside world only for preserving cans. While we were guests filming in their camp it was important to tread delicately in order not to offend their principles.

One day Elisabeth was sitting on the steps of the unit caravan, dressed in costume, cigarette in her mouth, painting her fingernails red, when a Hutterite woman happened to pass. Incensed by this spectacle, she snatched the cigarette, trampled it on the ground and smacked Elisabeth's face.

All hell broke loose. It was difficult to see who was the more outraged, the Hutterites at the affront to their customs, or Elisabeth at the insult to her status as film star. At first it looked as if we would be turned out, but eventually the leader of the community warned Elisabeth not to smoke in public, apportioned some of the blame to the woman, and allowed us to stay.

After finishing her part on location, Elisabeth went to New York with her husband, the director Dr Paul Czinner. When Michael Powell tried to contact her, she had disappeared. He traced her to Hollywood, but she claimed to be having trouble with her ears – or some such excuse – and refused to fly back to England. So we had to make do without her. Glynis Johns was given the part, which was filmed all in the studio using back projection.

By the time I flew back to England the Battle of Britain was over and bombing had started with a vengeance. At Waterloo station everything was blacked out, with just tiny pinpoints of light here and there. Noticing the potholes and broken glass, I wondered how on earth I was going to get to my home twenty miles away. Just then a taxi pulled up. 'Gerrards Cross?' said the driver. 'Right, guv.'

Like everyone else we got used to the Blitz. We bought yards and yards of blackout material for our house, which was Georgian with scores of windows and fanlights. A builder put up a dugout – an Anderson shelter – in the garden, with bunks. When there was an air-raid warning we followed a specially rigged-up rope in the dark, and slept there. From a food point of view we were fairly privileged. In Montreal I'd seen a sign in a

store urging people to send food parcels to their friends in England. I
went in and bought twelve months' supply of bacon, butter, sugar, etc.
Five years later it was still coming. In 1945 I sent them a cheque with
thanks for their generosity.

We gave a lot of parties in those days. Our friends were the actors
Clifford Mollinson and Jessie Matthews, whose big hit *Evergreen*
Marjorie had written, and the directors Victor Saville, Anthony Asquith
and Arthur Woods. We played charades – I'll always remember Victor
dressing up in shorts and my son's school blazer and cap – and spelling-
bees, which Anthony and Arthur always won.

Arthur, whom I worked with on *The Busman's Honeymoon*, was considered one of the most promising young directors. We were shocked
when he was killed in an air crash during training. Other colleagues were
also in action, including two members of my crew on *49th Parallel*: Skeets
Kelly and Henty Creer.

Henty joined the navy and was involved in hunting the *Tirpitz* when
his midget submarine was sunk. His mother, who was devoted to him,
refused to believe he was dead, and every summer after the war she spent
her fortnight's holiday in Norway, in the hope she would find him wandering round with amnesia.

Skeets too was reported missing, but this story has a happy ending. He
was in the Air Force Film Unit, and had the job of photographing bombing raids. On one of these he was shot down, believed killed, and I had the
sad task of writing his obituary in the *Daily Mail*. A year later we heard
he was safe. His Mosquito had come down in a wood. As instructed, they
set fire to the plane, escaped, and managed to make contact with the
Resistance. He was passed from one farmer to another on an escape route
which was supposed to end in his being picked up by the RAF. They
didn't get that far. Passing through Paris, he and a few other airmen found
themselves surrounded by the Gestapo, and he spent the rest of the war in
a POW camp.

In 1942 I finally got my chance to join the services. It came through an
approach from Thorold Dickinson. The army had commissioned
Thorold to make *Next of Kin*, a thriller with a message that proved popular not just with the services but on general release. After that he was
asked to form an Army Film Production Unit. He would be given the
rank of major; the director of each of the three units captain; his assistant
lieutenant; the operator sergeant; the focus puller corporal; the clapper
loader lance-corporal; and there would also be a number of privates. The

team of writers, organized on the same military principles, included Major Eric Ambler, Captain Carol Reed and Private Ustinov. As Chief Cameraman I went in as a captain. After a few months I became a director and head of a unit.

The first twelve months I spent at the camp at Barnard Castle in County Durham, where the school of infantry trained officers in the techniques of warfare. We produced training films to be shown to recruits all over the country. The military adviser was Colonel Wigram, Chief Instructor at the camp and brains of the training programme. He wrote the scripts, then out in the field I directed them with the help of a young major who corrected us on details of military procedure.

We filmed out on the moors, often using live ammunition. *Line Ahead* was a typical production. We filmed the troops advancing in single file with Bren guns firing between the lines and mortars going by overhead, then finishing the operation with hand-to-hand fighting in trenches.

Another film demonstrated the use of the phosphorus smoke bomb. In the script a tank appears over the brow of a hill, spots an MV anti-tank gun in a threatening position, and fires off a phosphorus shell, which lands in front of the gun, releasing a lot of smoke, so the tank has the chance to escape. The camera was set up in the position of the MV gun, so that the tank would be seen in long shot and the shell would explode just in front of us. Having finished our preparations, I called, 'Action!'

The tank appeared over the hill, and fired the shell. At that very moment it hit a bump, which projected its barrel upwards into a more vertical trajectory. Instead of landing a safe distance in front of us, the missile came down right beneath our noses.

We were knocked right off our feet, lacerated by hundreds of bits of metal, with this molten, flaming phosphorus stuff sticking to our skins. Ambulances rushed us to hospital, where we had treatment for burns. Fortunately no one was seriously injured. The main casualty, as far as I was concerned, was my brand new battledress, now in tatters. When I joined the army I had decided to do it in style, in a Savile Row uniform of elegant, light khaki. Its replacement was army issue, stiff as a plank, stinking of insecticide, and white-looking as if it had been thrown in a barrel of flour. To prevent it itching you had to soak it in water for hours before putting it on.

As film people we had our own way of working which didn't always jell with the army, particularly the Brigadier in charge of the camp. We were allocated various equipment and facilities: a truck for our props, a camera car and a four-seater for me and my assistants, a hut where we worked on animation at night. Soon after I arrived the Brigadier sent for me.

'Captain Young, I am informing you that from tomorrow all your vehicles will come under camp jurisdiction. When you want a car, you put in a chit, and if not otherwise required it will be made available for your use.'

I told him those were my vehicles, needed for the film unit.

'They are not *your* vehicles. And we are not in a film studio. Don't you understand, Captain Young, that you are now in the army? The vehicles will be taken over tomorrow. You are dismissed.'

I went straight back to my office and rang the Director of Army Kinematography. Later the Brigadier sent for me. 'How dare you go to the DAK?'

From this I gathered he'd received a bit of a rollocking from the DAK. I had outranked him, hence the pique. I said, 'Look, sir, although I'm only a captain on twelve pounds ten shillings a week, I gave up a jolly good job on more than ten times that amount to do this, because I thought it my duty.'

I wasn't going to be interfered with by some regular army brigadier. From that moment on I got the cold shoulder but at least he let me get on with my job.

I had no such problems with Colonel Wigram, a brilliant man who became a good friend. He was an expert on German warfare techniques, getting hold of their military manuals and studying them so as to invent counter-attacks. In 1944 he was posted to Italy and was tragically killed leading an attack.

Tubby Englander was my operator, and I managed to get two former colleagues, John Wilcox and Denys Coop, transferred from the navy, which was an unheard-of thing. Another member of the crew made a great impression on people wherever we went to film. This was Angela Martelli, to us the continuity girl but to the army a Regimental Sergeant Major and figure of great status.

Winston Churchill visited the camp more than once and watched us filming. I noticed that halfway round the tour they would take him into a hut and give him a brandy. He'd got it all laid on.

We filmed in dozens of camps, including Catterick and Aldershot. In Lulworth Cove, where we shot in Technicolor, the harbour was protected by a perforated pipeline which under attack could be filled with oil and set

Freddie photographs VIP visitor Winston Churchill at Barnard Castle army
camp, County Durham.

alight, stretching a ring of fire across the mouth of the cove. On the flat
beach of Troon in Scotland Combined Operations under Mountbatten
were practising troop landings for the invasion of France. Lorries emerged
from big doors in the bows of the ship, crashing through the surface of the
waves until they scraped on the sand. The trucks had pipes sticking up so
they could go underwater and still get air to the engine.

The work was incredibly hard, even for me, and after three years I got
so run down the army sent me to a Masonic hospital in Ravenscourt Park
that had given over half its beds for wounded officers. There I spent a
delightful ten days in bed being looked after by pretty VADs. It was
decided I should be invalided out, category C3, unfit for any future form
of military service. So I went home, relieved to be out of it. I felt I'd done
my bit.

8 *Caesar and Cleopatra*

I was hardly back a week when a call came from Denham studio. Shooting on George Bernard Shaw's *Caesar and Cleopatra* was held up because the cameraman, Bobby Krasker, was suffering from diabetes, and they wanted me to take over. I went to the studio and talked to the production team. I noticed Bobby didn't seem all that sorry to be pulling out. Then I met the director, Gabriel Pascal.

I had worked with Gaby briefly once before. Back in 1940 I was at a loose end, contracted to a film that was delayed, when I was telephoned by Captain Richard Norton, an executive with the company making Shaw's *Major Barbara*. 'Can you come down to Dorset?' he said. 'We're having a lot of problems with the photography. We keep getting scratches on the film.'

'What about Osmond?' Osmond Borrodaile was their cameraman, a Canadian famous for his location work for Zoltan Korda.

'Oh, he'll be delighted,' Norton reassured me. 'He's in deep trouble.'

I arrived late at night and was introduced to the co-directors, Gabriel Pascal and David Lean. In the morning there was still no sign of Osmond. I saw the rushes, which were indeed scratched. Later I heard Osmond had returned to London, which made me feel guilty and angry at being misled. But there wasn't anything I could do about it. In the film industry people do get hired and fired, often arbitrarily.

I checked the magazine and the gate of the camera and did some routine tests. Whether it was something I'd done or just plain luck, there was no more scratching. I worked on the film for two weeks and it was quite a happy experience. Gaby left most of the directing to David Lean. When I was recalled to London, I recommended Ronald Neame, and that was the beginning of Ronnie's long association with David, first as cameraman and then as producer.

Gaby was a plausible rogue. Arriving from his native Hungary claiming a romantic background as a gypsy and an officer of the Hussars, he turned up one day at Bernard Shaw's house in Ayot St Lawrence. A few

hours later he left, taking with him the film rights to all Shaw's plays and
the half-crown he needed for his taxi ride back to the station. At first he
mainly produced. *Pygmalion* (1938), directed by Anthony Asquith, and
Major Barbara were well received. Now J. Arthur Rank was giving him
close to a million pounds to produce and direct *Caesar and Cleopatra*.

Gaby was a showman and a charlatan and no good at all as a director.
He once asked me to photograph a 'close-up long shot'. He could be very
endearing – he invited me to be his blood brother – but this charm was, I
soon found, lost on his actors.

After only a week's shooting on *Caesar and Cleopatra* Vivien Leigh
was no longer on speaking terms with her director. Gaby would say to
me, 'Freddie, vill you ask Vivien if she vill valk jus a lil bit slow?'

Vivien was standing a couple of yards away, and I relayed the message.
'Yes,' she replied, 'but you tell Mr Pascal I shall do exactly as I please.' Or
words to that effect. Vivien was known for her salty tongue.

It was a mystery to me how relations had soured so quickly, but shortly
afterwards an incident revealed what it was like to work for Gaby. We
were using Technicolor, which required a lot of light, and when it came to
filming in a large set, the Council Chamber, we didn't have the equipment
to light more than half the set at a time. Knowing Vivien wasn't very well
and we would be unable to do any of her scenes the following day, I suggested she take the day off, and informed Gaby accordingly. When I
arrived next morning I was surprised to see Vivien in the middle of make-
up, which for the role of Cleopatra took about three hours. I said, 'What
are you doing here, Vivien?'

'You'd better ask Gaby.'

I found Gaby and demanded, 'Didn't you tell your assistant not to call
Vivien this morning?'

'Oh, Freddie, I clean forgot.'

We went through the whole film like this. Claude Rains felt the same,
although he was more diplomatic than Vivien. After a few days he
approached me and said, 'I have a problem, Freddie. You know my part is
supposed to be completed in twelve weeks? That's not very likely, is it?'

This was true. What with the ructions on set and constant interruptions
from air-raid warnings, we were already behind schedule.

'If it isn't,' said Claude, 'I'm in trouble . . .' He explained the deal that
Rank had made with the Government. They needed a star of Claude's
stature to sell the film in America, but in normal circumstances he
couldn't have afforded to work here because of our high rates of income

tax. The Inland Revenue had agreed to waive his tax liability provided he was out of the country within twelve weeks.

'I'll try and hurry things along,' I promised.

We managed to finish Claude's scenes with two days to spare. A few weeks later I received a small parcel containing a long gold cigarette lighter, the first ever made by Dunhill in that shape.

Gaby wanted to send a second unit to Egypt to film the battle scenes. J. Arthur Rank thought this unnecessary. However, Bernard Shaw's contract had stipulated that not one word of his screenplay was to be changed, and it was argued that fulfilment of this clause required the inclusion of footage from Egypt. Rank stuck to his position. Gaby appealed to the author, who fired off a provocative postcard. Dated 30 December 1944, it read:

> What!!! Cut out the first act!!! Throw Rains at the audience's head before it knows who he is, or where they are! Spoil a £300,000 ship for a ha'porth of tar?

Rank knew when he was beaten. He authorized the trip to Egypt.

The question then arose as to who should go. Gaby couldn't because he was officially an enemy alien. Next in line was Geoff Boothby, the assistant director, then Geoff was injured in a motor cycle accident. So I was asked to direct the unit in Egypt, and Rank gave me £1,000 for the extra responsibility. Ted Scaife, my operator, took over as cameraman.

The Egyptian army lent us a thousand troops and we filmed near the Pyramid at Mena. After shooting we retired to the comfort of the Grand Continental Hotel in Cairo and the soldiers camped out in the desert. During the day it was 110 degrees Fahrenheit but at night it got freezing cold, so the troops took to burning their wooden spears and papier mâché armour to keep warm. This was very annoying but there wasn't a lot we could do about it, other than ordering more armour from Cairo and hiding those soldiers without spears at the back of the ranks.

After a few weeks I received a telegram from the production manager in England, Tom White, to say very sorry, but the Government has given permission for Gaby to come out for forty-eight hours. Next day filming was interrupted by the sight of a Rolls-Royce speeding across the desert towards us. Out stepped a strangely garbed figure in jodhpurs and riding boots, a white jacket and red fez, carrying a gold-mounted cane.

'Hello, Freddie, how are you?' Gaby greeted me enthusiastically.

The interpreter, Lieutenant Niazi, was calling out instructions through a loudspeaker, moving the extras to their appointed positions. Gaby watched this for a while, then asked, 'Vat are these men doing?'

I explained the action taking place in that particular scene.

'Those men there. They have no spears or armour.'

I told him there was an unavoidable shortage of props.

'How come, Freddie? Why is this?'

I described the predicament of the Egyptian soldiers having to camp out in the freezing cold desert.

'Hmmph. And why –?'

'Look, Gaby, am I directing this or would you like to take over?'

'No, no, you carry on.'

Next day there happened to be a visit from a number of Egyptian Army top brass and their wives who had come to watch the filming. In the scene a troop of Ptolemy's soldiers were to come sweeping round the bottom of the hill on horseback. These extras were raw recruits who couldn't ride very well, and as it was a charge many of them fell off.

At this Gaby could restrain himself no longer. He grabbed the loud-speaker and yelled at the top of his voice, 'I am an officer of the Hungarian Hussars and you are a lot of Jewish bastards!'

There was a moment of dead silence. Then a few orders rang out and the Egyptian Army all formed up and marched away.

I turned to Gaby, seething. 'You've done it now, Gaby. That's just about the worst thing you could have said.'

I jumped into a Jeep and went tearing up the column. When I reached their leader I tried to reason with him.

'Captain Zaki? Captain Zaki?'

The captain gazed stonily into the distance.

'Captain Zaki, please stop . . .'

The Jeep lurched crazily across the desert as I vainly attempted to combine driving and persuasion.

'Please . . . Can't we talk about this?'

No response.

A mile further on we reached an old British Army camp that was their headquarters. They disappeared into the recesses of the officers' quarters. I tried to follow but the guards stopped me. After a while I was allowed in to resume my abject apologies. The film had already cost a million pounds, I pleaded. It was bringing a lot of foreign currency into Egypt. We had the co-operation of both the Egyptian and the British Governments. There would be a major diplomatic incident. I used every argument I could think of.

Freddie and director Gabriel Pascal (bare-chested) on location in Egypt for
Caesar and Cleopatra (1945). Looking over Pascal's left shoulder is Freddie's
assistant, Jack Cardiff.

Finally they said, 'If you get rid of that man Pascal, then we might consider coming back.' I returned to Gaby and gave him the hard word. Next
day he returned to England and filming continued.

It was interesting to compare this trip with my previous visit to Egypt in
1922, as assistant cameraman on *Fires of Fate*. Then it was a crew of a dozen
or so, a little camera on a tripod, and no lights or sound. Now there was a
small army of us, with lorries and generators and sophisticated equipment.
One thing that didn't change was the dragoman and contractor who sup-
plied us, then and now, with horses, tents and food. This was the Sheikh of
Mena. In 1922 the Sheikh had thrown a big party in the desert for us, with
a sheep roasted whole, and other delicacies and entertainments. Close to the
end of the desert schedule on *Caesar and Cleopatra* I noticed a group of
horsemen riding towards us. Judging from their fine robes, they were
important visitors, so I went over to greet them personally.

'Mr Freddie Young?'

'Yes?'

'The Sheikh of Mena would like to speak to you.'

I recognized the Sheikh immediately. He was a short man with a round face and a moustache. It was amazing that in twenty-two years he hardly seemed to have changed at all.

'My father often spoke of you,' said the Sheikh, 'of his pleasure at entertaining you on your last visit to Egypt. Now I too wish to invite you and your colleagues to share our hospitality.'

Freddie and his Australian assistant 'Bluey' Hill are visited by the Sheikh of Mena on the *Caesar and Cleopatra* shoot.

As he was speaking I realized this was the son of the old Sheikh, and I remembered now that as young men the two of us had spent some time together.

'Delighted,' I replied, 'but . . . all of us?'

He gestured expansively. 'Of course.'

On the agreed day half a dozen Daimler cars arrived at our hotel and the forty of us piled in. We followed a route through the desert illuminated by little flares in cans, and came to a group of marquees lit by fire lights and paraffin lamps. There was the same sumptuous spread, this time accompanied by dancing girls, gala gala men doing tricks, and a terrific display of Arabs dashing round on horses firing rifles in the air.

After this we left Cairo for Alexandria, making a detour through the site of the battlefield of El Alamein. The desert was littered with military debris. Despite the danger of unexploded mines, we couldn't resist taking photos of each other sitting in a burnt-out German Jeep.

In Alexandria we were to film Caesar's galley. This was built around an RAF launch with miniature oars two feet long and a dozen on each side, operated by one man hidden within the boat, and model soldiers a foot high, so that on screen the galley would appear enormous. When we tested the boat we found the last two oars in the stern weren't quite touching the water, but the special effects man said, 'Oh that's all right, we'll put a bit more ballast in the stern and that'll fix it.'

We couldn't shoot until the afternoon because we wanted a particular alignment of shadow, so I ordered the unit to be standing by at twelve-thirty and retired to my hotel room. I was suffering from a bit of Egyptian tummy at the time. Half an hour later I was lying there feeling like death when my assistant Bluey Hill burst into the room. 'Do you know what's happened?'

'Sure,' I replied. 'The galley's sunk.'

I knew his news had to be something terrible. Bluey explained that ballast had been put in the boat, then along came an unexpected swell and swamped it. The boat now lay in fifteen feet of water with just the top of the mast showing.

There was nothing to be done for ten days until they got the galley and props dried out, so I took the first RAF plane back to London. I told Gaby that the galley was the last shot and as soon as it was done we'd be finished.

Gaby said, 'Fine. But vile you vait for the galley I'd like some more shots of soldiers marching.'

'But Gaby, we've shot hours of that. It's ridiculous to go on shooting any more.'

'Vell, that's vat I vant.'

This was the last straw as far as I was concerned. 'I went out there to do my job,' I told him. 'I think I've done it very well. Now you're asking me to throw J. Arthur Rank's money down the drain. Well, I won't do it. I'm resigning.'

That was the end of my involvement with *Caesar and Cleopatra*. The unit in Egypt filmed the galley and, as requested, further footage of soldiers marching. The film was the most expensive made in Britain up to that time. A few years ago I saw it on television and there seemed to be hardly any location photography at all. As for Gaby, he moved to Hollywood to make another Shaw adaptation, *Androcles and the Lion*, and died shortly afterwards.

9 MGM

After the war I went to work for Metro-Goldwyn-Mayer as their Chief Cameraman in Britain. MGM bought the Amalgamated Studio in Borehamwood and completely revamped it, making it the most modern studio in the country. They raised the roof another fifteen feet, and replaced the air-conditioning with an alternative that used up less space. All facilities were on the same lavish scale. There was a metal shop and a carpenter's shop, making furniture for the offices and props and scenery for the three sound stages. These improvements took over a year and cost a million pounds.

I was given a whole corridor of rooms. I made the first one my office and the next, about forty feet long, the camera department. There were large metal cupboards, one for each of our three Mitchell cameras. The cameras were coded red, white and blue, and each of the hundreds of parts was marked with a spot in one of these colours so we didn't get the components muddled up. All the equipment came from MGM Culver City, except for items like blimps which were made in our own workshops. At the end of this corridor were wide doors so that the dollies, tracks and cameras could be wheeled straight out onto trucks when we went on location.

Running the camera department was quite a challenge, and I was always on the lookout for innovations to make it more efficient. It was unusual for the same man to be both head of the camera department and chief cameraman. My counterpart in Culver City had been a cameraman but now he was responsible only for the department, assigning equipment to the various units. The same was true over at Pinewood where the department was well run by Bert Easey. I tried to lure him over to MGM to work with me, but after some hesitation he decided to stay put – wisely, I think, because in the end his job lasted longer than mine.

MGM's reasons for making films in Britain were mainly financial. They had made a lot of money here that they couldn't repatriate because of currency control regulations, so they had to spend it somehow. The idea was they'd bring over an American director and a couple of Hollywood stars, and use British technical and acting talent. One of our early successes was *Ivanhoe*, with Robert Taylor, Elizabeth Taylor and Ava Gardner, directed by Richard Thorpe, which was the biggest-grossing MGM film of its year (1952) and gave me my first Oscar nomination.

The real star of *Ivanhoe* was perhaps the set. Sixty feet high and surrounded by a moat, the castle took months to build in the studio lot. After *Ivanhoe* certain details were changed so it could be used again on *Knights of the Round Table*, and over the next few years it appeared again in *The Black Prince* and several other pictures.

For the action sequences in *Ivanhoe* like the storming of the castle, we sometimes had hundreds of extras a day. Stunt men were drilled in the use of lances, spears, maces, longbows and crossbows. There was a machine that fired a few hundred arrows at a time so we could get the full effect of them raining down on the Norman defenders. In the most spectacular stunt, Paddy Ryan, one of the big names among British stunt men, was filmed falling in full armour from the top of the battlements all the way into the moat.

The man responsible for the stunts was Yakima Canutt. Yak was a legendary figure in Hollywood, a veteran stunt man who had started his career in 1912. His most famous work to date was *Stagecoach* where, doubling for John Wayne, he clambered forward over galloping horses to retrieve the reins. *Ivanhoe* was his first film in England. He showed our stunt men a lot of new tricks and I found it fascinating working with him. He told me how he once drove a team of six horses over an eighty-feet-high cliff into the sea. There was a special harness that released all the horses separately while he himself dived in a different direction. At the age of 56 he was retired from stunting and ran a team of stunt men that he'd trained himself. Each one specialized: one did falls, another swordfights, others car crashes, and so on.

For the jousting tournament in *Ivanhoe* Yakima had his own technique. The knight who was going to fall had a belt hidden under his armour, and attached to this was a thin wire invisible to the camera. The two knights galloped towards each other, and at the precise moment when the lance seemed to strike him the wire became taut and he was yanked backwards off his horse.

A few years later Yakima was to work on one of the most spectacular of stunt sequences, the chariot race in *Ben-Hur*, which took three months and cost millions. Many people thought it the best thing in the film. The director of this sequence was Andrew Marton, whom I met when we

Freddie in conference on *Ivanhoe* (1952).

worked together briefly on an Esther Williams picture, *One Piece Bathing Suit*. MGM wanted some shots of the Thames to use in Hollywood as back projection, and Andrew and I spent a couple of days on a tugboat photographing the river. Andrew was a gifted and intelligent man who felt he hadn't received the credit he deserved. In most films the stunts are filmed by a second unit with its own director, camera team, and doubles for the main actors. Second-unit cameramen and directors tend to get a raw deal. They often make a valuable contribution with little recognition because the real director doesn't like it to be known the film isn't all his own work.

By the early 1950s television in the States was catching on in a big way, and studio bosses tried everything they could think of – colour, spectacle, big budgets, exotic locations – in a desperate attempt to win their audience back. One such gimmick was 3-D.

In 1953 MGM decided 3-D was the coming thing. They got me to bring a couple of cameras over to Culver City, and while these were being converted for the new process we cameramen were given a course. Professors of optics explained the principle to us. The camera had two lenses and the distance between them could be adjusted: the bigger the gap the more things stood out on the screen.

I remember going to the cinema in Hollywood to see *The House of*

Wax, one of the first 3-D pictures. Watching the movie through these special Perspex glasses gave you the illusion you were being bombarded by objects flying straight at you. The audience went wild, shouting and screaming with laughter. Many years later I got to know the director of this film, André de Toth, when we spent a couple of days together on a recce in Leeds. The ironic thing is he was blind in one eye, which meant he couldn't have experienced for himself 3-D's stereoscopic effect.

3-D turned out to be a seven-day wonder. Apart from the manifold projection problems – it required two projectors – it gave some people in the audience a splitting headache. It was all right for people with perfect eyesight, but for those with one eye stronger than the other it was a great strain. So the idea was dropped and our cameras taken apart once more, this time to be converted to Cinemascope, an innovation that proved more durable.

The standard screen format used to be four by three – the same as a TV screen. In opting for a bigger screen the industry had to go wide: with a higher one, people sitting at the back of the stalls would have had the top of the image chopped off by the overhanging balcony. Cinemascope (and its successors, like Panavision) used anamorphic lenses on the camera and projector to squeeze the wider image onto a normal 35-mm film, and this gave a ratio of 2.35:1. Early 'scope lenses tended to distort, and we were told not to do close-ups. A face in the centre of the screen would come out fat, and one on the edges thin, so close-ups had to be framed a bit off-centre. By the end of the 1950s lenses were much improved and this was no longer a problem.

Starting with *Knights of the Round Table* (1954) most of my films at MGM were in 'Scope. The format wasn't always helpful. *Lust for Life* (1956) included a lot of shots of Vincent van Gogh's paintings. Since the pictures tended to be longer in the vertical it was tough framing them with a higher screen. I think we ended up having to pan up and down.

Discussions went on for some years about what one should do with Cinemascope. Great for westerns, it was generally agreed, but how do you frame an ordinary domestic drama? In *The Barretts of Wimpole Street* (1957) the set of the Georgian town house was designed by our art director, Alfred Junge. To make the room look wider he gave it two windows, and extra-broad antique furniture was found. Then the director, Sidney Franklin, didn't like the windows and they were replaced by a single one. In those days there was always this peculiar struggle going on between directors and art directors about the wide format. Over time these conversations didn't happen any more. We simply got used to it.

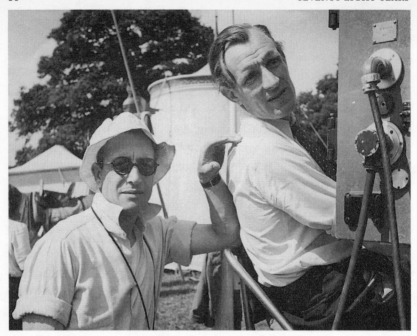

Freddie with his great friend and colleague, Skeets Kelly.

At Elstree I had about ten assistants, so we could field two or three units at the same time. My main operator was my old friend Skeets Kelly. Skeets was an engaging personality, a great story-teller, a natural and spontaneous man. In the 1930s the film business used to be much more formal. It was always Mr Wilcox, Mr Young – nowadays it's Freddie or Chuck or Butch. When he started as a clapper loader at British and Dominions Skeets was a tall, skinny boy of fifteen. One day he noticed a man leaning against a rostrum flicking through some stills, so he wandered over to take a look for himself, casually putting his arm round the man's neck and leaning over his shoulder. Herbert Wilcox turned to see who it was taking this unaccustomed liberty. Suddenly recognizing his boss, Skeets jumped like a scared rabbit and fled. We didn't see him for the rest of the day.

Skeets had now been in the industry twenty years and he was still an operator. From time to time the Head of Production at Elstree, Ben Goetz, would say, 'We need a cameraman to do a picture on "B" stage and you're tied up on "A" stage. Who do you recommend?' I'd reply, 'What about Skeets? Time you gave him a chance.' Ben would shake his head. 'We've got to have a reputable cameraman. We can't afford to risk someone young and inexperienced.'

Finally MGM made a picture in India called *Soldiers Three*, and during editing they found they needed some extra scenes. I said to Goetz, 'Look, this is an ideal chance for Skeets. I guarantee he'll make a good job of it,' and Goetz relented. In the canteen we had a table for the cameramen and when Skeets came in I gave him the news. 'Oh, great!' he exclaimed. A bit later Ben entered and Skeets jumped up and thrust out his hand. 'Thank you, Mr Goetz, for giving me this great opportunity and I promise you I'll do my best.' Ben hardly paused in his stride. 'You'd better,' he growled, continuing on to the executive table.

Next Monday I was busy lighting on 'A' stage when in rushed a worried-looking Skeets. 'Freddie,' he burst out, 'I'm in a bell tent. I don't know where to start.'

I excused myself to my director and went to 'B' stage. On the set was a complete bell tent, about ten feet wide, with three actors inside. I thought for a moment. 'Cut off the top of the tent and put a little rail up there with three or four lamps that you can spot down on the different actors. Outside the tent if you place a brute [a very powerful arc light] to shine through the canvas that'll make it luminous like daylight.'

I left him and he did as suggested. Bell tents are hardly in the run of things even for an experienced lighting cameraman, and to have this problem thrust on you on your first day must have been unnerving. Skeets completed the scenes and the producer expressed himself satisfied with the work. After this, Skeets went back to operating, no further opportunities arose, and in the end I said to him, 'Look, Skeets, you'll just have to take a gamble. Leave MGM and try your luck outside.' That's what he did, and later became successful as a second-unit cameraman.

I made several trips to Hollywood on MGM business. Once I was introduced to Louis B. Mayer himself; he gave me a limp, perfunctory handshake and passed on to the next person. It was always interesting to watch the company's lavish production methods and to meet other cameramen, such as Joe Ruttenberg and Charlie Rosher. Charlie was an Englishman who had run a portrait studio in Bond Street before going out to Hollywood. Out there they loved to make fun of limeys. Instead of the usual canvas chair on set Charlie had a special one with a sumptuous velvet seat. One day he returned from lunch to find some wit had inscribed on it 'Lord Plushbottom'.

I watched them filming the musical *Showboat*. Charlie was supposed to be the director of photography, but to speed things up they had two other top cameramen working with him. When they finished shooting on one set the actors and director moved to another that was all ready for them. Joe Ruttenberg had lit it, and all Charlie had to do was change a couple of diffusers, just as a gesture, so he was ready to go in five minutes. After that they went to a third set, prepared by another famous cameraman. You couldn't afford to do that in England, but they were all under contract and I suppose the studio didn't need them for any other work on that particular day.

Out on the lot they had a hundred-yard stretch flooded to about five feet and in this was a mock-up of the paddle-steamer as if floating on the Mississippi River. Below the surface of the water a steel cable was attached to a winch. The camera rolled, the paddles revolved, and the boat moved away from camera with Howard Keel waving goodbye to Ava Gardner on shore. Considering they could also use location footage from the Mississippi, this was a fantastic set to have on the lot for just one little scene.

I had been invited to join the American Society of Cinematographers, and I very much admired this organization and the way it offered a forum for members to meet and discuss technical and aesthetic matters. Some of us in Britain thought it would be a good idea to form our own Society. The Association of Cinematograph and Television Technicians (ACTT) got to hear of this, so two or three of us met George Elvin, general secretary of the union, at the Round House pub in Wardour Street.

'We're not keen on the idea,' Elvyn said. 'We think it'll take authority away from the union.'

'Not at all,' we replied. 'It has nothing to do with the union. The union will still represent us over money, employment, working conditions. The BSC is going to be different. Members will get together and talk about lighting and cameras and things like that.'

'Nevertheless, we don't want you to do it.'

'Well, we're going to do it whether you like it or not.'

And on that note the meeting broke up.

The British Society of Cinematographers was founded in 1949 with about sixty members, among them Ossie Morris, Jack Hildyard, Harry Waxman and Bert Easey. It was decided that membership would be by invitation only to cameramen with at least three credits for feature films. We also invited some technical people, like George Gunn of Technicolor and, later, Sydney Samuelson. I was elected President for the first three years, 1949–51. We met once a month with a guest of honour who spoke on a particular topic. An early guest was Sir Russell Flint, the water-colourist, who talked about the relationship between painting and lighting.

When I visited Hollywood I was always interested in their techniques, which at the time were way ahead of ours. One thing that impressed me was the Hollywood grips system. A camera grip is someone who helps out with camera movement, laying the tracks, pushing the dolly, etc. In Hollywood there is another kind of grip, who is a general-purpose technician, part electrician, part carpenter. The latter has no equivalent in Britain where traditionally the unions have insisted on those functions being carried out by specialists. I took my gaffer (chief electrician) Cyril Cambridge with me to Hollywood to take a look at the grips system. Back home we got union permission to try it out on one film. Unfortunately, after that the union decided to ban it.

As Chief Cameraman at MGM I was doing a similar job to the one at British and Dominions before the war. In other ways the set-up was completely different. The budgets were much bigger. Herbert Wilcox didn't skimp on production values, but the apparent opulence of his films flattered the actual cost of the sets and the fast shooting schedule. MGM, on the other hand, were truly extravagant. At British and Dominions we were more of a team; there were the same three or four house directors – Herbert himself, or Jack Raymond – and although Herbert hired a number of foreign stars and technicians, they came on his terms. At MGM, the Anglo-American relationship was different: it was an American company with American producers, so inevitably there was a bit of conflict.

They found our British trade union practices restrictive. If a director wanted to do an hour's overtime he'd have to go round asking each member of the unit if he'd agree to stay. In Hollywood things like that are much more casual. But then American technicians were much better paid, generally owned cars, and didn't have to face the problems of commuting by public transport to a studio twenty miles out of town. So this objection wasn't very fair.

Directors used to get irritated with our tea breaks. 'Ah, you guys,' they'd say. 'Always drinking tea.' 'Its just the same in Hollywood,' I'd reply, 'except there you drink coffee.'

The boss of MGM in Britain was Ben Goetz, who was the brother of L. B. Mayer's son-in-law. A lot of directors used to make snide remarks about him: his cushy job, the suite of rooms at Claridge's, the chauffeur-driven car and the American salary on expenses in Britain. It was said that he was just a figurehead at Elstree, that he couldn't lift a finger without permission from Culver City. He was a shrewd businessman, in fact, but what he didn't know about films would fill a book.

On location for *Bhowani Junction* (1956): by the blimped camera with Freddie are Nicolas Roeg (kneeling) and Stewart Granger (with hand on Roeg's head).

From time to time he would comment on my work, 'Ava Gardner's face – it's all dark.'

'Yes, it's meant to be. She's in silhouette against the window.'

'We pay her a lot of money, Freddie. I wanna see her face on the screen.'

'Well, perhaps you'd better get yourself another cameraman. Because that's the way I see it.'

Ben would pat me on the shoulder and say, 'I was only joking, Freddie.'

You mustn't let yourself be pushed around by these executives, no matter how big they are, if you want to protect your reputation as a cameraman.

From time to time MGM made some pretty stupid decisions. *Bhowani Junction* (1957), set in India during the war, was about racial tension and Indian nationalism. Ava Gardner played (convincingly) an Anglo-Indian girl who has three suitors: an Indian (Francis Matthews), an English colonel (Stewart Granger), and Anglo-Indian (Bill Travers). These three actors were all white and British. After some to-ing and fro-ing between the three men, she finally concludes that she is trapped within her own caste, and settles for her old Anglo-Indian sweetheart.

We spent a month filming around the railway station and marshalling yards of Lahore, and everyone was pleased with the result. In fact, I received a telegram from Dore Schary, the head of production at Culver City, congratulating me on the photography, and the whole crew on the marvellous job of work they'd done.

Then MGM sneak-previewed the film in front of an audience of students in San Francisco. On such occasions the audience are given cards on which they are asked to record their reactions to the film. Many of them objected to the outcome – to the liaison between 'an American girl' and an Indian. Ava Gardner can't marry a black, was their verdict.

MGM panicked. Fearing a flop and damage to the reputation of their star, they called on the director, George Cukor, to retake the ending, making Ava marry the English colonel. George refused. Schary said, 'You'll do it, or you'll never work for MGM again.' That was the typical threat that studio executives used to make in those days. So George reluctantly submitted. To my mind this new ending ruined the whole film.

I spent almost fifteen years at MGM. They had a fine studio at Elstree, but they under-used it. With good organization they could have shot two or three films at a time. In fact there was seldom more than one stage in use, and long periods when they weren't making anything. It was a shame to see such waste. After I left, the studio carried on for a few years before closing down in the early 1970s.

10 How was I, Freddie?

In my films for MGM typically the director and a couple of stars would be American, and the rest of the cast and crew British. I think it's not unfair to say that Hollywood stars expected a more pampered treatment. We heard that in Hollywood at the end of a take it was the custom for the crew to applaud. When Greer Garson came over in 1945 to do the sequel to *Mrs Miniver*, the focus puller was one of my young assistants, Christopher Doll. After one very emotional take Greer Garson noticed Chris wiping tears from his eyes.

'Oh, you dear boy!' she exclaimed. 'How kind.'

Chris loved to send people up. He should have been an actor himself.

I got some idea of the power of the star from the first film we made at Elstree after the studio was converted. This was *Edward, My Son* (1948), directed by George Cukor and starring Deborah Kerr and Spencer Tracy.

During this period there was a craze for long takes; on the next stage Hitchcock was doing the same thing with *Under Capricorn*. Long takes give an actor more opportunity to develop his performance and for a cameraman too they are an exciting thing to do. However, there are good reasons why this technique is not used more often. Unless the material is very strong, a long, static take can get quite boring – other angles could be cut in during editing, but in that case there wouldn't have been any point doing a long take in the first place – so one usually plans a certain amount of movement within the shot, for both the players and the camera. This creates problems with sound and lighting. For the sound man there is the nightmare of where to put his microphone, unless the sound is post-synched, which nobody likes doing if it can be helped. And the cameraman has to choose between lighting acres of set, losing atmosphere and subtlety, or having a complicated series of light cues, dimming lamps up and down, which can easily go wrong. All in all we found long takes a lot more trouble than they were worth, and within a few months the idea had gone out of fashion.

I have very enjoyable memories of Spencer Tracy. He was a wonderful

Freddie with Spencer Tracy and George Cukor in the making of *Edward, My Son* (1948).

chap to work with, a natural actor. These long takes didn't trouble him at all. If he couldn't remember his lines he'd just rub his nose and say something that seemed to make sense. He never dried up. We had been told by Dore Schary that Spence had been ill so we must treat him gently, working only a five-hour day. On one particular day we were to do a ten-minute take with the camera on a crane moving the whole time. We lit the set and practised the camera moves while the actors rehearsed. Then George Cukor said, 'All right, let's have a go.'

For once everything went without a hitch. At the end George said, 'Cut! How was it for you, Freddie?'

'Fine.'

'Sound?'

'No problem.'

'You happy, Spence?'

'OK'

'Right,' said George. 'Great. Print it.'

Spence walked across the stage and picked up his hat.

'Hey, where are you going?' asked George.

'I'm going home. You said it was fine. You can't use two takes, can you?' And Spence walked through the door and out of the studio.

George nearly exploded. It was true that he only needed one take but directors always like to cover themselves by getting two or three in case there is a scratch on the film or some other unforeseen problem. But Spencer Tracy was a big star at MGM and supposed to be a convalescent so there wasn't much he could do about it.

I got on very well with Spence. At the end of the film he said to me, 'You must come over to Hollywood and direct my next film.'

'Thanks very much. I'd love to.'

I never heard from him again.

On my visits to Los Angeles I got the chance to see the Hollywood star in his own habitat, as it were. Walking through the Culver City lot one day with Cyril Cambridge, my gaffer from Elstree, I bumped into Walter Pidgeon, whom I knew through working with him on a Bulldog Drummond picture a couple of years before.

'Hello, my dear boy,' he drawled. 'What are you doing here? Well, you must have dinner with us . . . Where are you staying? I'll come and pick you up.'

Next evening at seven a long, sleek Cadillac pulled up outside our hotel. 'Here we are, boys, jump in.' Walter's mansion was pure Beverly Hills: swimming pool, immaculate floodlit garden, black butler, etc. Other guests arrived and we drank Martinis mixed American style, very dry. Over dinner Walter stood up and raised his champagne glass.

'I should like to propose a toast to the greatest man in the world, Winston Churchill.'

It seemed to me I should reciprocate this gesture so, remembering the famous wartime alliance, I raised my glass. 'To another marvellous man, Mr Roosevelt.'

'That son of a bitch!' exclaimed Walter. 'He ruined me.'

I looked round at the luxurious house and garden, the retinue of servants, the eight-course dinner table. 'But Walter, you don't look like a ruined man to me.'

On location too nothing but the best will do. On *Solomon and Sheba* (1959) Tyrone Power arrived in Spain, bringing with him on the liner his own yacht, which was then berthed in the south of France. On Saturday night, at the end of a week's work, he would fly from Madrid and spend Sunday on his yacht, returning twenty-four hours later. It seemed crazy to me, flying all that way just for twenty-four hours.

Ty seemed healthy. As he was still an army reserve, he had his annual medical at the camp, and was passed one hundred per cent fit. A few days

Freddie with Tyrone Power (left of picture).

later he was doing a sword fight with George Sanders at the studio in Madrid. It was the middle of winter, and freezing cold out on the lot. I noticed Ty's legs were mauve with the cold. Ty said to King Vidor, the director, 'I feel terrible.'

King excused him to go to his caravan and take a rest, and we continued shooting on George Sanders. A few minutes later we were told that Ty was dead.

So much for the medical, which failed to pick up Ty's heart condition. A few days later I witnessed my first Hollywood-style funeral, with Ty's widow sitting next to the coffin of her embalmed husband in his blue suit and gold wrist-watch, arms crossed over his chest. Some days afterwards I was sitting near George Sanders, who was reading a letter. George burst out laughing. 'Just listen to this, Freddie . . .'

The letter described Ty's second funeral in Hollywood. There was the same filing past the coffin, except this time with music – 'I'll see you in my dreams', or some such old favourite – with Merle Oberon wearing the Chinese costume from the movie she was filming at the time, and all the other stars dressed up to the nines. George, who had a sardonic sense of humour, was much amused by this macabre description.

At this point the film was almost finished, although lacking certain crucial scenes. We had to shoot the whole thing again, this time with Yul Brynner. In the battle scenes Ty had worn a red bandanna, and King Vidor hoped to use the long shots. Yul Brynner refused point-blank to wear this bandanna, so that was that. It occurred to us that Yul did that to ensure there was no trace at all of his predecessor in the completed film.

Actors are very dependent on the cameraman. Hollywood cameramen like to tell the story of the star who marries a millionaire, retires, then fifteen years later, after the divorce, decides to make her comeback. The studio agrees. She says, 'But of course I must have Joe.' Joe is her favourite cameraman, whom she's always relied on to make her look beautiful with little tricks of lighting. They do some tests and next day they view the rushes. She looks at herself on the screen, turns to Joe and says, 'Joe, you don't make me look as good as you used to.' 'Well, darling,' he replies, 'you see, I'm fifteen years older now.'

It's happened to me scores of times that an actor comes up to me after the take and asks, 'How was I, Freddie?' 'Fine,' I reply. 'I have to ask,' they explain, 'because the director never tells me anything. I never know whether he's happy or not.'

Tact is of the essence. On *Goodbye, Mr Chips* Greer Garson was thirty and it was her first film. MGM had signed her up the year before and then left her kicking her heels in Hollywood for months until a suitable vehicle came up. It was important for her to make a good impression. During the first day or two I noticed she was giggling a lot out of nervousness with Robert Donat in between takes. Greer had a delightful, twinkling laugh, and her ease with Bob was obviously helping her performance, but it made things difficult for me because her make-up was looking messy and her mascara running from laughing so much. I took her aside and spoke to her, and after that she soon settled down.

Goodbye, Mr Chips was the first film I did for MGM, back in 1938, when I was still under contract to Herbert Wilcox. There was a huge cast of schoolboys; since the film covers sixty years of a schoolmaster's career we had to have relays of boys to play them. Of all the pictures I've worked on, I'd say *Goodbye, Mr Chips*, along with *Doctor Zhivago*, were my personal favourites. At the end of filming Robert Donat gave me a beautiful and unusual picture of a group of ballet dancers, a ninon collage.

I made four films with Bob, including his last one, *The Inn of the Sixth Happiness*, in which he played the part of an old mandarin. A few days before the end of filming he had a brain haemorrhage and when he returned to the studio he was a sick man. He was unable to remember his lines, and these had to be written on boards placed before the camera. It was very sad. I remember going to the toilet one day and standing next to Bob. I glanced round and there were tears running down his cheeks.

'Oh, Freddie, I'm so ashamed.'

'But Bob, you're doing a marvellous job. You've been ill and I think you're terribly plucky to come in. Most actors would have stayed at home, and here you are trying hard to get the picture finished.'

I think I managed to make him feel a bit better. The same day we finished shooting on him. One of his last lines to Ingrid Bergman was, 'I don't think we shall meet again, my dear.' The next day the unit moved to Wales for location shooting. A few days later we heard that Bob had died.

The Inn of the Sixth Happiness was about the missionary in China, Gladys Aylward. Filming the story required a number of improvisations. The slopes of Snowdonia had to be set on fire to turn the green bracken brown like the hills of China. To play a Chinese character Curt Jurgens was given brown contact lenses and a crew-cut wig. As for Ingrid, you couldn't call a film *The Small Woman* (the title of the book on which the film was based, by Alan Burgess) when your leading lady was five feet ten.

Freddie with Ingrid Bergman on location for *The Inn of the Sixth Happiness* (1958). Lighting his cigarette left of picture is Mark Robson.

Ingrid was a warm, generous person. At the end of *Indiscreet* (1958) there was a luncheon party at a restaurant in Borehamwood, after which we were to return to the studio to watch a rough cut of the film. While we were waiting for the first course, Ingrid pulled out a long box and presented it to me. It was a French corkscrew and six-inch carving knife, suitable for a picnic and beautifully made out of stag's horn. I took out a sixpence and gave it to Ingrid, saying, 'It's bad luck to accept a sharp instrument without giving a coin in return. Didn't you know?'

I tried out the knife, pressing a button to open it, then another to close it – right over my thumb. It went in deep, right through to the joint, almost severing it, and blood spurted all over the table.

Ingrid's husband Lars took control of the situation. He wrapped a napkin round my thumb and dashed me off to casualty in his car. Fortunately the injury wasn't as bad as I'd feared. They put in seven stitches, and I was able to return to the studio. In the projection room Ingrid beckoned to me.

'Come here, Freddie. I've kept a place for you next to me.' She'd gone to the trouble of ordering a basket of food and champagne from the restaurant, and I watched the rest of the film tucking into this.

After that, I didn't see Ingrid again until 1981. Sydney Samuelson rang me up and asked, 'Are you free to do a little job?' At his camera-hire business in Cricklewood, Sydney had a small studio and cutting rooms, mainly used for commercials, called Production Village. 'Some American producers are here and they want to do a test on Ingrid Bergman for the role of Golda Meir.'

At the studio Ingrid rushed over to greet me. 'Oh, Freddie, how nice to see a face I know.'

Ingrid had insisted on doing the test, which is a most unusual thing for a big star. Most of them would consider it beneath their dignity. She wanted to convince herself that she was right for the part. I can see why: who would have thought of Ingrid – a fair-haired, blue-eyed, Swede – as Golda Meir? We did three different make-ups, at forty-five years old, fifty-five, then seventy. I thought she was very good, and the Americans were delighted. I didn't realize then that she had cancer. I heard later she suffered a lot from the heat in Israel. At the end of the film she returned to England for more treatment, and died shortly afterwards.

As a cameraman you have to acquire certain odd skills. One of these is throwing things. If you want a shot of someone being hit by an object – the classic custard pie, for example – the aim and the timing have to be perfect. In *I Accuse* (1957), we were filming a scene in Brussels (standing in for Paris, at the time of the Dreyfus affair). In the scene a disreputable chap comes along the road wheeling a barrow of second-hand books; when he reaches a Jewish butcher's shop he seizes a book, hurls it through the window and runs away.

José Ferrer, the director, had cast an extra, but then we had doubts whether he would do it right. Normally in such scenes you use sugar glass in a frame of yucca wood, but on this occasion it was a real plate-glass window. If the timing was wrong and the glass failed to smash in an appropriately spectacular manner, we would lose a lot of time and money. It was decided I should do it.

I disappeared behind the sound truck and they dressed me up in corduroy trousers, a sailor's peaked cap, an old overcoat and scarf, and I was given a droopy walrus moustache. Only José and the make-up man knew about this. I decided to play a little joke.

I sidled up to the camera and took a squint through the lens. 'Bugger off!' I was told, and the boys elbowed me out of the way. I went up to Dora Wright, the production manager and quite an important lady, stood close to her and started rubbing up against her arm. 'Get away, you filthy beast!' she cried.

When it was time for the shot I came up the road with my barrow, smashed the window and hared off. Then I returned to the camera, whipped off my moustache and revealed myself. That got a big laugh.

Completing a film at all, let alone on time and on budget, and to the high standards you've set yourselves, requires utter ruthlessness. Sometimes the odd joke can release some of that tension. And sometimes a film-maker has to perform himself to keep control of his project.

In 1941 I photographed *The Young Mr Pitt* for Carol Reed. Carol was known to be a very slow director. When a film is falling behind schedule, it's often the cameraman who's blamed for hold-ups. In my experience this is rarely true.

The normal practice on a set is first the actors do a run-through, and the director comments on performance, pace, etc. The camera crew are also watching, and I might have something to say, like, 'How about starting on a long shot, with the door opening?', and the operator might suggest a track at a certain point. These ideas are bounced back and forth, then there's a second run-through. When the director is satisfied, then it's up to the camera crew and the grips to lay the track and do the lighting. You have to consider the time of day, whether there's supposed to be daylight coming in through a window, or it's night-time and which lights are on in the room, also the atmosphere of the scene itself. It might take us an hour or more to get ready, then there's another rehearsal with all the lighting and the camera movements. There may be one or two further changes: the director might alter a line of dialogue, or the precise moment when the camera has to move in close; an actor might be unhappy about a gesture he's been called on to do. All this is agreed, and you finally shoot it.

Some cameramen light faster than others, but in nine cases out of ten when time is wasted, it's not because the cameraman has been slow but because the director has been indecisive in working out how to shoot the scene or, when it is shot, has insisted on an inordinate number of takes.

Carol Reed had his own way of directing. He used to work at his own pace, and he didn't stand on dignity. One day, coming out of the studio at lunch-time, he said, 'Race you to the pub for a quid.' I won. He wasn't much faster at running than he was at making films. On set he would walk up and down with Bob Donat discussing how to play the scene, then he'd sit down, smoke a cigarette, and meanwhile we would all be ready and waiting to go.

A week into the film the producer, Ted Black, complained that we were already two days behind schedule. 'Don't blame me,' I told him. 'It's the director who sets the speed of shooting. You talk to Carol.'

Afterwards, Carol said to me, 'Don't worry, Freddie. What you're doing is beautiful. Just carry on as usual. I have an infallible method for these producers who want to hurry things up.'

'What's that, Carol? What do you do?'

'I let tears come into my eyes, and I look terribly upset, and before long the producer's got his arm round me, saying, "It's all right, Carol. You leave the worry to me, let me take care of it." And I always get away with it. It's the only way to deal with producers.'

Carol was an actor before he took up directing.

During my time at MGM I worked for a certain director who used to call us to order, shouting 'I'm the director! I'm the director!' This exclamation created great hilarity amongst the crew. Obviously, the need to demand respect showed he had already lost it. When a director knows what he's about the crew automatically senses it, and responds accordingly. I never heard David Lean raise his voice on set.

Freddie and Richard Brooks on location for *Lord Jim*.

In the public imagination the director is an eccentric figure – megalomaniac and exhibitionist, larger than life. I suppose we ourselves are responsible for the stereotype because, from silent days onwards, movies about film-making have tended to show the director as this type of character. But sometimes directors are a bit like that. I recall Gaby Pascal on *Caesar and Cleopatra* turning up in the desert with his red fez and gold-mounted cane. Cutting a dash, dressed for the part. The director.

In 1964 I worked with Richard Brooks on *Lord Jim*. Richard had a mania for secrecy. He was loth to give me a script and when he did I had to swear not to divulge the contents to anyone, not even my nearest and dearest. At the end of filming he collected the scripts from those favoured few who'd been allowed to have one. I couldn't see what was so unique about the story. It was a hotpotch of every film you've ever seen: a bit of piracy, mysticism, love interest – and anyway, anyone wanting to know needed only to read the original novel by Joseph Conrad. I could only suppose that as a writer he'd had his ideas stolen before.

The rushes were also guarded with the tightest security. The only people allowed to see them were myself, the sound man and the editors. Actors were strictly forbidden. He even wanted the projectionist's port-hole pasted up. When it was pointed out that the projectionist needed to check that the film was in rack and in focus, he relented, though reluctantly. After the viewing he made sure of the rushes by taking them home with him.

Richard wore heavy climbing boots and trousers two inches short. He perspired continuously, and always had his shirt wide open as if he needed all the air he could get to fuel his violent rages. On set he was brusque, aggressive and unpredictable. Once he asked for a pencil to mark the script, and someone handed him a yellow one. Richard lost his temper, breaking the pencil and throwing away the bits.

However, he did have a sense of humour. The morning after a day when he'd been particularly vocal a group of us gathered in the foyer of the Hong Kong hotel before leaving for work. Among the unit were two props men called Chuck and Bobby, who always went around together. When Richard came out of the lift, he announced croakily, 'I think I'm losing my voice.'

'Well, thank God for that,' remarked Chuck.

I expected Richard to blow his top, but he joined in the joke against himself.

While we were shooting *Lord Jim* there was another unit making a film of us at work. Richard always carried a whistle to attract people's attention and to start or stop the action. When the documentary was finished we were all invited to a viewing. The director had given it an apt title: *Shooting by the Whistle*.

Richard was really more bark than bite. Having more energy than patience, he was abrasive but not malicious. In a long and prolific career he has directed some fine films. Even if his working methods are a bit odd, one respects that. After all, it's the product that counts.

Directors welcome suggestions, so long as they're able to believe they thought of them themselves. I once said to a director, 'Don't you think it would be a good idea if we did such and such,' and he replied, 'No, no, my dear boy, it wouldn't work.' Five minutes later he said, 'I've just had a bright idea. We'll do it this way.' Exactly what I'd just told him. It was so blatant I could hardly believe it.

Before taking charge of a film, a director might have been a producer, an assistant director, a stage director, an editor, an actor, a writer or indeed a cameraman. In some cases he might rarely have set foot in a studio before, and need a lot of help from his cameraman. With an inexperienced director, the cameraman can be effectively the co-director. He wants you to tell him what to do, but not in a way that compromises his authority. It's a bit like a rookie lieutenant and his battle-hardened NCO. As the film progresses and the director gets more confidence, he might start to resent this dependence. He can be easily offended, and you find yourself walking a fine line.

Gottfried Reinhardt (son of Max) was originally a writer/producer for MGM. *Betrayed* (1954) was his first film as director. The story concerned the betrayal of the British Army by a Dutch traitor at the time of Arnhem. We were filming in Holland on a country road, dead straight for half a mile on either side, lined by a hedge and behind that market gardens. Five hundred Dutch soldiers dressed in British uniforms were standing by as we prepared a long tracking shot with our two stars, Clark Gable and Lana Turner, who were supposed to be straggling back from the war zone, in the foreground.

Tracking shots always take some time to line up, with the camera grips using spirit levels and wedges to get the track absolutely level. The lighting was also quite delicate because the scene was taking place at dawn with mist. Finally we were ready to shoot. But there was no sign of the director. Reinhardt was a great gourmet and he'd gone off somewhere for lunch. When he turned up, I said, 'Gottfried, we'd better get cracking because it's already three o'clock and it'll be dark in an hour.'

He gave me a sharp look and didn't reply straight away. Then he said, 'I want the track moved.'

'What for?'

'I don't like the position. I think I'll have it over there.' He pointed to a spot a hundred yards down the road.

'What's the difference, Gottfried? The road's exactly the same. I've got a brute out there in the cabbage field on a rostrum. By the time we've moved it, it'll be too late to get the shot today.'

'I don't care about that. I want it moved.' He turned on his heel and walked off.

So the five hundred troops had to be engaged for another day, at a cost of several thousand pounds, just in order to move a track from one piece of road to another identical piece of road. But the director is all-powerful, you can't argue with him if he wants to be obstinate like that. He must have felt that my reaction on his return from lunch contained an implicit criticism. Which I suppose it did.

In 1955 I worked with Vincente Minnelli on *Lust for Life*, a biography of Van Gogh. Minnelli had started his career in the art department as a set dresser, and this showed in his attention to the minutiae of the set, even down to the knives and forks on the table. This was not a bad quality on a picture like this, where pictorial detail was so important, but one can go too far.

There is a scene near the end, when Van Gogh is painting in a field of wheat, just before he shoots himself. We had bought a wheat field from a farmer, cut a furrow through to make a road, and placed a cherry tree in the foreground. The tree was mature, and weighed several tons. Planting it was a major operation, requiring us to dig a huge hole and ease it in with a crane, before filling in the earth and replacing the surrounding vegetation. The tree was so top-heavy with leaves and branches it had to be supported with piano wires to prevent it falling over.

When this was done we lined up the camera so that the framing exactly reproduced what Van Gogh would have seen when he was painting the picture.

Minnelli came along and looked through the lens. 'No, no.' He shook his head. 'It's not right.'

'What's the matter?'

'The tree's in the wrong place. We'll move it three feet to the left.'

'Why not just move the camera? It comes to exactly the same thing.'

Vince insisted, 'It has to be the tree.'

'That means we'll lose a whole day's work, Vince. Not to mention the cost.'

Vince was adamant. The men lifted the tree out, moved it a yard, put it

On the set of *Lust for Life* (1954): Freddie is right of picture, second row. Centre, above the clapperboard, is Vincente Minnelli and, to his right, Kirk Douglas.

back in. It fell over, lost a couple of branches, a few thousand leaves. If we'd moved the camera a few inches instead of shifting this great big tree a yard, the image would have been just the same.

Some years later I worked with Liza Minnelli on a show for American TV, filmed on the stage of the Rainbow, Finsbury Park. I told her I'd photographed *Lust For Life*. She exclaimed, 'Oh, that's my Dad's favourite picture!'

I liked it too. For a cameraman it was especially interesting. MGM did a beautiful job reproducing Van Gogh's pictures. We filmed in Holland, Belgium, Paris, Arles – the actual places where the painter had lived and worked. Wherever we went we filmed in real rooms in period houses, or built sets near the location. The asylum in the picture is the same one where Van Gogh was a patient. It had been derelict for years and we had to clean it up before we could start filming. The grounds looked as if they hadn't been touched since the day he was there.

One scene showed the family of Belgian peasants depicted in the painting, *The Potato Eaters*. The art director decorated the set exactly as it looked in the painting, with an oil lamp hanging over the table, then I had to match the lighting. It was an enjoyable thing to do, like painting a picture. Casting the extras was no problem – people in that part of Belgium still have those same gaunt, craggy faces – and we had the advantage of an actor, Kirk Douglas, who was the spitting image of Van Gogh himself.

Some directors want to do your job for you, while others, like George Cukor, concentrate entirely on the actors. It amuses me to read reviews of George's films, praising his intelligent choice of angles and so on, knowing that George never even used to look through the camera.

On *Bhowani Junction* (1955) we were in Pakistan, filming around a railway station. The idea was to give the impression of the main characters living in the midst of this great mass of people, and in practically every exterior we had hundreds of extras in the background. This wasn't difficult to arrange because if you hire a few people and start shooting, you can bet your life about a thousand onlookers will turn up to see what you're doing.

One day we were on a rostrum doing a scene with Ava Gardner in the foreground. As we were about to shoot, George suddenly called out, 'Hold it!'

He jumped down and forced his way through the crowd to a spot fifty yards away. George always used to carry a few pages of the script for that day's work, and he'd roll these up into a scroll. He stopped in front of a particular individual, one of thousands in those long white robes all Pakistanis wear, and to our amazement he started berating this chap, shouting and beating him about the head with his script. The man was one of those simple-minded fellows who have a perpetual smile on their faces. He probably didn't understand a word George was saying.

George struggled back through the milling throng, red in the face, panting, still fuming with rage.

'What's up, George? we asked, unable to contain our laughter.

'He was looking straight at the camera. And smiling.'

'But George, from this distance you can't tell if he's smiling or crying. His face is about the size of a pinhead in the camera. And anyway, he's entitled to be there. We're not paying him.'

'I don't care,' George growled. 'Son-of-a-bitch shouldn't look at the camera.'

If the director doesn't look through the camera from time to time, he doesn't know these things. It's the same with sound. I've often found with directors that the slightest noise, like someone coughing or a car back-firing, will put him off his stride, and he'll shout at his assistant, 'Stop that god-damn noise!' Really he should have more faith in his sound man, and his cameraman, that they'll tell him if it's going to make any difference. Directors shouldn't be over-concerned with these matters, but they're always highly strung, particularly if things aren't going too well.

Some people would say it's the easiest thing in the world to direct. With a workable script, competent actors and a good cameraman, all the director has to do is shout 'Action!' and 'Cut!' And, indeed, good films have been made despite having to carry an incompetent director. On the other hand a great director is someone with the vision and inspiration to weld the skills of his collaborators into something greater than the sum of its parts. One thinks, for example, of David Lean in *Lawrence of Arabia* and the sheer will and stamina to sustain a team through a two-year slog on location. Another director who impressed me was John Ford.

Mogambo (1953) was a remake of the 1932 *Red Dust*, with Clark Gable (who was also in the original) being pursued on safari by Ava Gardner and Grace Kelly. Robert Surtees had photographed the location stuff in Africa, then the cast came to Elstree to complete the film, with me as cameraman. It turned out they hadn't done much work out there, and most of the film was shot in the studio with location footage used as back projection. Fortunately, the head gardener was a clever horticulturist, and he transformed the set into a jungle with exotic trees. In the warm, damp atmosphere the plants thrived for several weeks.

John Ford later said in an interview he agreed to direct *Mogambo* because he hadn't been to that part of Africa before. Certainly it was well known that if John didn't like a story he didn't take too much trouble over it. Be that as it may, I remember thinking at the time he knew his job all right. One always gets an impression of whether a director knows what he's doing or whether he's unsure of himself. Ford was masterly, he knew exactly what he wanted, he never hummed and hawed over the set-up. He'd stand on set and say, 'Take it from here. Full-length figure,' making a shape with his hands. Then he'd go to a tighter shot above the knees, followed by close-ups. He'd already worked out which shot to do on which line of dialogue.

Freddie with Clark Gable and John Ford, talking about the making of *Mogambo*.

He told me, 'I only shoot what I want to use, to stop the bastards re-cutting the film afterwards.' The custom at MGM was to allow the director the first cut, then the studio would have a look at the film and edit it again themselves. But with a John Ford movie they couldn't do that. There was no footage left for anyone to re-edit in a different way.

John didn't look through the camera. He didn't even like viewing rushes. And he never tracked or panned if he could help it, believing that camera movement was disconcerting for the audience. He saw each shot as a separate picture: he'd start a scene with a group composition then cut from one static set-up to another. It was a crisp style of directing and cutting. A lot of young directors move the camera all the time. They've seen tracking shots done by other directors and they think that's a clever thing to do. To them it seems dull just to cut from one shot to another. But sometimes a simple cut, which shows a direct cause and effect, is more effective. Because, truly, acting is the greater part of a film. If a picture is poorly acted the critics might say it's beautifully photographed. But generally speaking it's the story, not the photography, that's of supreme importance. In fact, I've seen successful films rather badly photographed.

John had a reputation for being cruel. An actor once asked (so I've heard), 'How do you want me to play this scene, Mr Ford?' John replied, 'Hell, you're the actor, you act. You do it.' He would have said that just for a bit of quiet laughter to himself, or to amuse the unit. When I was photographing *The Tamarind Seed* for Blake Edwards in 1973 the conversation turned to John Ford. Blake told me:

'I made a film with Ford once. I was a young man then and terrifically keen. We were on this remote Pacific island and I was an extra. One day after shooting everyone was packing up and John was sitting alone, so I seized the opportunity of having a word with him. "Hello, Mr Ford" – and I introduced myself – "I just got out of the army. I'm very fit, ready to do anything. Any time you want any stunts doing . . . I'm your man."

'John Ford looked me up and down. "Sure. Climb that tree."

'I looked round and there was this big palm tree. So I shinned up it. I was wearing shorts and my arms and legs were scratched to bits by the rough bark. After a great struggle I got to the top. I looked down to see what Ford wanted me to do next. And there was no one there. The island was deserted. Then I looked out to sea and I saw Ford and the rest of the unit on their way to the mainland in a motor boat.

'So I had to clamber down again, and row across to the mainland – at least he'd left me with a rowboat – and I got back sunburnt, blistered, scratched, dying of thirst. But I'll tell you one thing, Freddie, it taught me a lesson I'll never forget – not to approach a man like Ford with a foolish offer like that.'

John could certainly be irascible. He'd lost the sight in one eye, which he covered with a black patch. On set he'd sit there chewing on a handkerchief, looking morose. On *Gideon's Day* (1958) we had a disagreement about something and were hardly on speaking terms for a couple of days. We were sitting in the back of a car on the way to a location and I was thinking what a stubborn man he was, when he said, 'I've not been feeling too good. My eye's been giving me a lot of trouble.'

I realized that in his oblique way he was trying to make it up. In a moment the ice was broken and we were good friends again. Once you broke through his reserve John was a lovely old chap.

Lawrence of Arabia (1962): Freddie and David Lean confer over the viewfinder.

In 1959 I had been with MGM fifteen years. When my contract was about to expire I went to see Matthew Raymond, the studio manager. I reminded him they had to give me six weeks' notice of renewal and that period had now arrived.

'We don't want to lose you,' he said, 'but things are a bit tight. We were wondering if you'd consider taking a reduction in salary?'

I said no. All the years I'd been with MGM they'd lent me to other companies – United Artists, Columbia, Paramount, British Lion – for double my salary, so I felt it was a bit of a cheek to ask me that, considering I'd cost them practically nothing.

So I left MGM and went freelance. For a few weeks I was completely lost. Nobody contacted me. I was an MGM man out of touch with the rest of the film world. Then a couple of small pictures came my way, I shot the first of over a hundred TV commercials I've done over the years, and a few months later there was a phone call from Sam Spiegel. David Lean was preparing to make a film about T. E. Lawrence: was I free to photograph it?

I knew David Lean from his time in the cutting room – he had edited several of my films, including *49th Parallel* – and from my few days' work on *Major Barbara*, his first directing credit. Now he was the top British director, and about to tackle a subject that just about everyone in the industry had been wanting to film for the past forty years.

The first thing was to go to Jordan to recce the desert locations. With the set designer John Bryan and assistant director Gerry O'Hara I flew to Petra, where a group of Arabs escorted us through the gorge on horse-back. By the time we got back the warm sunshine had given way to a bitterly cold dusk. Soon after this John and Gerry resigned, both of them because of kidney trouble. I think all of us had realized it was going to be a very tough picture.

Back in London David Lean and I discussed how *Lawrence* would be filmed. David wanted to use 65-mm cameras, instead of the normal 35-mm, because the finer grain of the 70-mm film would give the desert scenes superior definition. He also told me he wanted to photograph a mirage. At the time I had no idea how I was to do it.

No shot in *Lawrence* – or perhaps in any film I've photographed – has received as much attention as the mirage. I found the solution when I went to Hollywood to select the camera equipment. Robert Gottschalk, President of Panavision, was showing me round his plant, when I noticed a long 500-mm telephoto lens. A mirage in the desert is always seen in the distance, looking as though the sea is lying on top of the sand. With a telephoto you can film this in close-up, which enables the audience to see details of the heatwave and the blueness invisible to the naked eye.

The shot was carefully prepared. One sees mirages in the desert almost daily, but they are not a reliable phenomenon. It depends, I suppose, on the kind of terrain, the wind conditions, other factors. We chose a spot which we knew normally produced a mirage at the hottest time of the day. There we built a dummy well. Lawrence and his Arab friend, who is drawing water, were in the foreground, and Omar Sharif, on his camel, was placed a quarter of a mile in the distance. At a given signal the camera rolled and Sharif's camel began trotting forward. We shot a thousand feet (about ten minutes), ending with the arrival of camel and rider at the well.

On the screen you see first just the mirage, then on the horizon a shimmering dot of a figure. As he comes closer you get a distorted image of his camel trotting, it seems, through water, and finally a clear view of Omar Sharif approaching the last few yards. Screen time is less than ten minutes, because David cut to reaction shots of the two men at the well getting more and more tense, right up to the moment when Omar shoots the other Arab. It is not just the photography but also the sound – the clop-clop of the camel's hooves – and the rhythm of the editing that make this such an effective scene.

Freddie nurses the mighty lens used for Lawrence's mirage scene, with the film's restorer Bob Harris.

Telephoto lenses – although not as long as this one – have been around since the 1920s, and many people have looked at a mirage through binoculars, but I believe this was the first time anyone had photographed one this way. Since then I've seen it done dozens of times.

While I was at Panavision Bob Gottschalk told me he was looking for an agency in the UK to handle his camera equipment. I immediately thought of my old friends the Samuelson brothers – David, Sydney, Michael and Tony – who ran a camera-hire business at Cricklewood. Their father Bertie Samuelson was a producer at Walton Hall Studio in Isleworth, where I shot my first film *Victory* in the 1920s. The sons followed similar careers to mine, leaving school at fourteen and becoming newsreel cameramen, before going on to other things. When I told Sydney I'd mentioned his name, he took the first plane out to Los Angeles, and this is how Samuelsons' became the UK agent for Panavision.

The location headquarters, offices and workshops were at Aqaba in Jordan, but the first six months were spent at a camp hundreds of miles away in the heart of the desert. Despite the remoteness, conditions were not Spartan. Apart from David Lean, who had a caravan, we were all in tents, but these were double clad, with camp-beds, chairs, a washstand and even a canvas bath which the local attendants filled for you every evening. There was an enormous refrigeration truck for the thousands of feet of film, some of which was taken out every evening to warm up overnight, and for the fresh food, beer and ice. Another tent housed the well-stocked bar, and in a marquee Location Caterers served bacon and eggs for breakfast, and a full-scale dinner with fresh meat, vegetables and fruit.

The unit had its own twenty-seater Dove aircraft, used for bringing in supplies from Jerusalem, Beirut and Amman, and for sending exposed film on the first stage of the journey to London every evening for processing. It was always an anxious moment when we got the cabled report back from the laboratory forty-eight hours later. From time to time the plane took us out for a break in a hotel with air-conditioning and a swimming pool, and once we were invited to dinner on Sam Spiegel's yacht off Beirut.

One day we were watching the arrival of a Jordanian Air plane when someone noticed the pilot had forgotten to lower the undercarriage. It hit the ground, skidded along on its belly for fifty yards, and ground to a halt. The door slowly opened and Tony Quinn emerged, looking like a man in a dream. No one was injured.

At the request of King Hussein thousands of Arabs, together with their families, camels, tents, goats, etc., had travelled hundreds of miles to the location. Organizing them was a slow business. Just as you were about to shoot, one of them would wander off and relieve themselves. Then another would kneel down to pray. One had to be patient. They were doing us a favour; it wasn't like dealing with hired extras in England.

We had 100 vehicles, including thirty Jeeps, to move the 200 technicians and actors. There was a quarter of a mile of miniature railway track, with its own electric crane, large enough for lamps and crew, that could travel up to 30 m.p.h. We used this to film moving shots of men on camels. At its full height of nine feet you could be eye level with the rider.

The second crane was a Chapman, an eight-wheeled truck with large pneumatic tyres and an elevation of thirty feet, which was often necessary for long shots on undulating ground. It could travel on relatively soft sand that had been flattened and rolled. We used this for the charge on Aqaba, where the camera follows the attacking camels for a couple of hundred yards. This vehicle was petrol-driven and therefore noisy, so you had to take a separate soundtrack.

The camera truck, designed by Skeets Kelly, was a large van containing racks for equipment, a darkroom, even a toilet, and on the front was a hydraulic lift that would take the camera up to fifteen feet.

Sand would penetrate everything, and we had an air-conditioned truck where the cameras could be cleaned and serviced. During the day we were plagued by dust storms and flying insects. With temperatures of 110 degrees Fahrenheit we protected the cameras with sunshades and covered them with damp cloths to keep them cool. Shooting at night it got so cold we put electric heaters in the cameras so the motors didn't slow down. We'd sip hot soup, while the Arabs huddled round fires boiling tea.

The heat didn't bother us too much because it was dry heat and one's perspiration immediately evaporated. Most people on a film spend a lot of time standing around waiting – but not the camera team. No one works harder than a cameraman. Being so busy I found myself less sensitive to the hardships than some people in the unit.

One particular day we were filming the scene where Lawrence's Arab friend is killed in the quicksand. First we had to climb up a thirty-feet sand dune. This may not sound so difficult. But the sand of the desert is fine and loose, and you tend to sink up to the knees at every step. I was thinking about lighting. Even in blinding sunshine you need filler light or the faces would be too dark to see their expressions. At the top I said to

David, 'We'll never manage to get any brutes up here. We'll have to make do with a couple of reflectors.'

We spent the day up the dune doing the scene. Meanwhile the electricians, with nothing to do because we weren't using any lights, stayed behind in a tent smoking and playing cards. One of them had a heart attack. He was rushed to the camp and flown back to England where he recovered. I always felt that if he'd been actively involved, as I was, instead of sitting in a tent smoking, he might have been all right.

Apart from this incident, and one or two cases of sunstroke, there was very little illness. It was a hard life in the desert, but strangely beautiful and exhilarating.

We often shot at sunrise or sunset – the magic hour, as film people call it, for at this time you can get some striking effects. Being closer to the equator, the period of twilight was only about fifteen minutes – so everything had to be rehearsed and ready. We then had to drive back to the camp in darkness, negotiating hazardous bumps and ravines along the way. The nights were usually starry, but still you had to keep in convoy. Just following a track you could easily get lost, and being left behind in the desert overnight without food or drink is no joke.

We seldom shot anywhere near the camp, as David was a stickler for finding precise and varied scenery for every sequence in the film. You approached the shooting area with great care. All vehicles had to stay out of sight behind a declivity some distance away. If one careless driver ran through the foreground, wheel marks had to be obliterated by brushing and scraping, which wasted a lot of time. The desert had to be virginal, with not even a camel track to be seen until the camels entered the frame. We had to watch out even when eating our lunch, because if a plastic cup or paper bag were blown into the picture it was no easy matter to retrieve it without leaving footprints in the sand.

Preparing a tracking shot would sometimes take a whole day, rolling the sand, laying the track, and so on. The position was chosen in advance, and then a gang would carry out the work the day before shooting. Then a sandstorm might blow up overnight, and the track would be covered a foot deep, taking hours to dig out.

A lot of things came up in shooting that we could use. Light conditions were always changing, and spirals of sand, called dust devils, would spring up from the desert, whirled by hot currents of air, and travel rapidly at us in a long sideways column, taking sunshades and other paraphernalia with them. Mirages appeared from time to time, and we were able to shoot

Freddie on his hands and knees for sand-smoothing duties on *Lawrence of Arabia.*

close shots with telephoto lenses, showing camel riders apparently walking up to their knees in water, elongated and quivering into odd shapes.
These moments contribute an atmosphere of unreality to the finished
film.

Sometimes on a film you find yourself thinking, God, this is a boring,
obvious way to shoot this scene. With David it was never like that. I
always felt that what I was doing was good and fresh. He inspired you to
go out of your depth and try and do something extraordinary. He was
very keen on pictorial things, and yet I never felt he was trying to do my
job for me.

The compositions were worked out between us. For example, one shot
early in the film starts with the camera low down, and all you see is sand
stretching away to infinity. Then you see the backs of the camels' legs
going past the camera – plop, plop, plop – and as they pass over a rise the
camera rises on the crane to disclose an endless vista of the desert beyond.
We worked out the set-up together, then it was David who suggested the
embellishment of having the camera go up.

He was meticulous in arranging a set-up. There were discussions with
the art director, the camera operator, myself. He was very open. Sometimes
he'd say to a carpenter, 'What do you think? How would you do this
scene?' More often than not the chippie retreated, terrified, muttering, 'Oh,
I don't know, Mr Lean', but sometimes he gave an opinion, and David
would reply, 'Good idea. Let's do that', or 'Thanks, but I don't think that's
quite right.' He'd listen to anyone, but he himself was the final arbiter.

Although he took a lot of time to make a film, David was neither indecisive nor wasteful. He used most of what he shot. Some directors shoot
masses of stuff from different angles, hoping it'll all cut together in the
end. But David wasn't like that. Once having decided how to play the
scene, he shot it in that one way, with few, if any, covering shots. He had
the mind of a trained editor, knowing as he shot what he expected to see
on the screen. I agree with this. I think there's only one best way of doing
a scene. It might involve considerable thought and preparation, but it's
better to first work out your conception and then stick to it.

After six months in Jordan Sam Spiegel moved the unit to Spain, where
we did the interiors in various Moorish buildings in Seville, such as the
headquarters of the Spanish Army, the Alcazar and the Duque de Alba's
Palace. John Box, the art director, embellished those rooms to resemble
Allenby's headquarters in Cairo, Jerusalem and Damascus.

Interior locations create their own special problems. Throughout a

Lawrence of Arabia.

day's work the sun moves round, clouds come and go, and to maintain even continuity from one take to another you have to keep correcting the lighting to compensate for the changing light quality coming in through the windows. In a studio there is air-conditioning and soundproofing, whereas on a location the windows must be kept shut to exclude street noises, so things get fearfully hot. You also have to take great care with the curtains, carpets, etc., which can easily be damaged by the heat from the lights. Despite all this, you get a realism beyond even the best studio facilities.

After the interiors we filmed the sequences of trains being attacked by Lawrence and the Arabs. At Almeria there was an isolated stretch of sand dunes similar to some of the locations we used in Jordan. There we built two miles of railway track, and brought in engines and carriages. At the time Almeria consisted of just a few old-fashioned hotels and fishermen's cottages. Now it's a thriving tourist resort, but I'm told the desert areas are still much in demand by film companies, and the oasis we made for *Lawrence* has been used in many other pictures.

The Aqaba sequence was also shot at Almeria. At the sea front we built the facias of the buildings of the town. For the charge by the Arabs on the Turkish defenders we needed a long, straight section for the tracking shot from the Chapman truck. The sand was bulldozed flat, then wetted and rolled flat to make a smooth surface. Another shot in this scene has Lawrence walking by the sea at dusk. As this was the Mediterranean – the east – coast of Spain, we shot it at dawn, using pink filtering to accentuate the roseate quality of sunset.

While we were filming in Spain there was a near-catastrophe. The vehicles were parked in a dried-up river bed. During a break the continuity girl and I were having a discussion with David in his caravan. It had started to rain, but no one paid much attention. A few moments later someone glanced out of the window. The trickle of water in the river bed had turned into a torrent. Water was up to the axles and about to come in under the door.

Props man Eddie Fowlie saved the day. He jumped into a Jeep, ploughed through the water to the caravan door, and the three of us clambered in and were driven to safety. It was touch and go. But for Eddie's presence of mind and driving skill we could easily have been swept away. A couple of generators and various vehicles were submerged, and it was a couple of days before they could be recovered.

After Spain we went to Morocco to film the 'bloodbath' sequence when the Turkish Army is massacred. David always took his Rolls-Royce wherever he was working, and he asked me to join him on the trip. The drive over the Atlas mountains was marvellous, but our new base at Wadi Zat was hot, dusty and miserable. We weren't surprised to learn it was where the French Foreign Legion used to send its soldiers as a punishment. For this scene, and the other major battle scene, the attack on Aqaba, we had two or three cameras but no second unit, which David disliked, preferring to direct every shot himself.

At the end of filming David asked me to stay on and supervise the processing, making sure that all the original colours of the desert, which varied from black through red and yellow to almost white, came out in the finished print. Altogether my work on the film lasted two years, from 1960 to 1962. And that was the end of making *Lawrence of Arabia*.

Well, not quite the end. A few months later I was in Malaysia doing location work for *The 7th Dawn*, a story about the Emergency of 1948. One day we were filming on a stretch of beach where the jungle ran almost to the water's edge. In the scene William Holden, playing a rubber planter, spots the MG of the British Resident's daughter (Susannah York). He walks out along a tree trunk overhanging the water and shouts, 'Come out of the water, you young fool! Don't you know there are guerrillas in the area?', and she replies, 'I can't. I'm not wearing anything. You'll have to throw me my things.'

At midday most of us ate by the roadside, but Bill Holden and Lewis Gilbert, the director, disappeared somewhere in a car. After lunch we lined up the shot and got everything ready, but there was no sign of Lewis and Bill. I asked the assistant director, 'What's happened? Where have they gone?'

'I think they went to a hotel.'

I glanced at the sky. It was looking a bit squally, and I wondered if there might be another shower. 'How far is this hotel?'

I was getting more and more restive. Finally the car returned and Bill and Lewis got out. They looked rather casual and were smiling as if pleased with themselves about something.

'We're all ready,' I said. 'Bill, when you walk out on that tree trunk we've made a cross where you stop and say your line.'

'OK, Freddie.'

Lewis looked through the camera and said, 'All right, shall we rehearse? Action, Bill.'

Bill came out on the tree and stopped at the mark. He hesitated. Then he pulled out a piece of paper. Oh, God, I thought, now he can't remember his lines. I was getting very fed up. Bill looked at the paper and read out:

'Academy Award. Best photography: *Lawrence of Arabia*. Freddie Young.'

The whole unit erupted into cheers and gathered round to congratulate me. That evening we celebrated with champagne. Bill and Lewis had gone to the trouble of driving all that way so they could phone Hollywood and get the results of the Oscars. Meanwhile I'd been thinking, What the hell are they doing? We should be getting on with the filming. I was very touched. I'd completely forgotten about the Oscars.

The Oscar was accepted on my behalf in Hollywood and sent to me. Some time later, when I was selling my flat, a lady came round from the estate agency. She noticed the Oscar and asked, 'What's this?'

Freddie receives glad tidings of Oscar glory on location for *The Seventh Dawn*
(1964).

'It's an Oscar. For *Lawrence of Arabia*.'

'Oh, *Lawrence of Arabia*! I've seen it three times.'

'Oh, good. I'm glad you enjoyed it.'

'Yes. I loved the music.'

I preferred David Lean's interpretation. 'The music and the photography always go together,' he told me. 'It's the combination that people respond to. Her liking the music is really a great compliment to the photography.'

While I was in Malaysia I received a telegram from my long-lost brother Bill, saying he was ill in hospital in Papua New Guinea and didn't expect to live long. I wired back, urging him to hang on till I'd finished the picture.

I travelled on a complicated route via Singapore, Brisbane, and then on a twenty-seater plane to Port Moresby. All the while I was thinking of Bill. He was eighteen months older than me, and probably the one of my seven brothers and sisters I had been closest to. When we were children he used to call me 'diamond nose' and I called him 'splosh'. Like myself, he worked at Gaumont for a time, as an assistant props or something. Bill was a bit of a rolling stone, never settling down to any job for very long. I'd spent my whole life as a cameraman based in England, while he'd emigrated to Australia in the 1920s, then moved around the Far East, ending up in New Guinea. I felt our lives had taken very different courses.

At Port Moresby we landed on a cricket pitch with a pavilion at the side. A crowd of locals was sitting by the airfield watching. I suppose it must have been a big event in their lives seeing a plane arrive. As I walked towards the pavilion I noticed a chap in a tropical suit eyeing the passengers intently. It looked like Bill, but I couldn't be sure because I hadn't seen him for forty years.

I walked right up to him and stopped. He was looking straight past me at the other passengers. Tapping him on the shoulder, I said, 'Hello, Bill.'

He looked round. 'Freddie!'

He hadn't recognized me. My hair was now white, and I suppose he must still have had this image of me as a skinny kid of nineteen.

Bill took me to a rest house where he'd booked a room. We opened a bottle of whisky that I'd brought, and had a drink. I was sitting on the bed, and Bill on a chair, and we started talking about the things that we'd done and hadn't done. Eventually a great wave of tiredness came over me and I said, 'Bill, I haven't slept for forty-eight hours. I'll have to shut my eyes for a minute or so.'

I lay down on the bed and went straight to sleep. I must have been out for a good three or four hours. When I awoke there was an inch left in the whisky bottle, and Bill was sitting in the same position, devouring me with his eyes.

'Well, Bill, what are we going to do?'

'I want you to come to the hospital with me, and meet my doctors and nurses.

The medical staff told me how much Bill had been longing for my visit. Without that he probably would have died several weeks ago. He had a tumour in his stomach.

I could only stay a couple of days because my wife was now danger-ously ill. Marjorie had suffered from cancer for many years, and we had endured the all-too-familiar story of sudden crises, false hopes and grad-ual decline. A few weeks after I got home I had a letter from a Mr Stock in New Guinea. Bill had discharged himself from hospital, and travelled 200 miles up river to manage this man's copra plantation. And there Bill had died. Mr Stock buried him next to his own son.

Shortly after this Marjorie died too. After her funeral I moved out of the Brighton flat as fast as I could, and I plunged myself into work.

13 The Snow in Spain

Three years later I photographed my second film for David Lean. Of all the pictures I've worked on, I think *Doctor Zhivago* is the most memorable and challenging. It has an enormous variety of mood and situation, and Omar Sharif and Julie Christie as the lovers are just right. I thought Julie was quite stunning. Although she's not terribly striking if you see her on the street, she's marvellously photogenic and comes alive when she's acting. The film is of course a love story, and David did everything possible to create the right atmosphere on set, even to the extent of playing a record of Russian balalaika music during rehearsals.

I've often been asked in which part of Russia we filmed *Zhivago*. The fact is that apart from a few minutes' screen time done by a second unit in Finland, the whole of the film was shot in Spain. My second wife Joan's uncle and aunt, who lived in Russia until their twenties, found it absolutely convincing, and the Russian film executives I met when working in Leningrad in 1974 were also complimentary.

Audiences don't realize – they're not meant to – that much of the snow in the picture is not snow at all. Filming lasted a year, so obviously some of the winter scenes had to be photographed in warmer weather. The coldest place in Spain is Soria, four hours' drive north of Madrid, but when we got there we found only a light covering of snow and the furrows plainly visible in the ploughed fields. The solution to this was marble dust. We bought hundreds of tons from a local marble works, and spread it on the ground. Hedgerows in the distance were draped with white plastic sheets, and whitewash was sprayed on the trees. I think we managed a passable imitation of the Russian landscape in the depths of winter.

Make-up was tricky too. When the Rod Steiger character enters a building covered in snow, we used rock salt on his coat and shaving cream on his beard.

The art department did a terrific job on the house at Varykino – the ice palace, we called it – where Zhivago and Lara isolate themselves for a few

Doctor Zhivago (Omar Sharif) sees through a glass frostily.

months. Plaster was used to create the effect of snow and ice, and the ici-cles were made of candle grease. I photographed this with a blue filter to give it an extra coldness.

The train sequence was done in the Madrid studio on a wagon set mounted on springs and rocked by a couple of camera grips. When the characters open the door to leave, they find a sheet of ice across the open-ing, which Zhivago breaks with a shovel. The ice was made of candle wax. Inside the wagon there is a brazier, which the characters huddle around swathed in scarves and furs. We felt sorry for the actors. Underneath these heavy clothes they were absolutely boiling.

In another scene the Red Army charges across a frozen lake. Some of them get shot, and the horses tumble and slither across the ice. The art department bulldozed a piece of land flat, and sprinkled marble dust on it to resemble snow-covered ice. Certain patches were given a layer of soap. When the stunt man reached this slippery spot, he pulled the reins in a certain way, and animal and rider skidded along the 'ice'. No one would believe it wasn't a frozen lake.

One effect that defeated us was simulating breath in the cold air. You can do this for a couple of seconds by the actor inhaling cigarette smoke, then at the right moment breathing out. For a longer take that's impossible. But if you manage to create an atmosphere where the audience believes it's freezing cold, they won't notice if not every detail is absolutely right. Film-making is all illusion.

Two symbolic details in *Zhivago* that just about everyone noticed were the daffodils and the leaves. The daffodils were grown in greenhouses until they reached bud, then they were rushed up to Soria and planted out in their hundreds. We had to juggle the schedule so that at the crucial moment we were on the spot and ready to do those scenes.

On location, creating the scenic splendour of *Doctor Zhivago*.

Doctor Zhivago: Zhivago (Omar Sharif) has his first vision of Lara (Julie Christie).

In the autumn the property department collected tons of leaves and put them in sacks. When the time came, they were scattered on the ground and a wind machine was used to create a flurry. In the scene outside the library where Lara works, David Lean wanted the leaves to swirl in a circular motion, to indicate not only a feeling of sadness from the autumn leaves but also the confusion of thoughts in the characters' minds. To get this whirlpool effect a ring of pipes was placed just under the ground with air blowing out at strategic points.

All this shows the lengths to which David would go to create an effect. It cost a great deal of time and money but without that I don't think *Zhivago* would have become such a huge success.

Outside Madrid they built a street set a quarter of a mile long with the facades of a few dozen houses, and one more or less complete building where Zhivago's family lived. We also had a real tram. The high voltage made this hazardous and we had an expert standing by all the time. Seeing the sparks fly from the junction of the cable and the arm of the tram took my mind back to the old days when there were trams in England.

There are a couple of touches in *Zhivago* I'm quite proud of. The first

is when Zhivago first notices Lara. After Lara's mother has taken an over-
dose, Zhivago wanders into the dimly lit machine room of her house, then
glances through an inside window. All he sees is a woman's hand, picked
out in the dark. Then Komorovsky (Rod Steiger) enters through a far
door, switches on the light, and we see Lara, who's been sitting in the
dark. David Lean has often complimented me on this scene and the effect
of the spotlight on the hand. A few years later he wrote to me: 'An almost
black screen and a lighted hand. It was your idea completely. Very daring.
Not realistic. Magic. Sensual delight.'

The other inspiration was using a vignette on Omar Sharif. A vignette
is a halo effect, a close-up of a face ringed by a fuzziness at the edges of the
frame. You get this by stretching a piece of white gauze over the camera a
few inches in front of the lens, then using a lighted cigarette to burn a hole
in the centre of the gauze. In the old days a star like Greta Garbo might be
photographed in this way to make her look more beautiful. The technique
is now out of fashion, though once in a while one reverts to old tricks,
when there is a leading lady no longer quite so young, for instance. On
Zhivago the purpose of this shot was dramatic.

After wandering around in the snow for days, Zhivago arrives at Lara's
house. He looks in the mirror and this blotched, haggard face stares back
at him. We framed Omar's head in the hole in the gauze, then flooded the
gauze with light from the front, taking care not to hit the lens. The result
is everything appears white except Omar's face. The viewers' attention is
concentrated on the face, and they share the character's horrified reaction
to his own appearance.

Towards the end of the schedule in Madrid, we experienced a real-life
drama. My wife Joan, who was seven months pregnant, suddenly went
into labour.

I had first met Joan the previous year in Hong Kong filming *Lord Jim*.
On Christmas Eve the continuity girl Angela Martelli, an old friend and
colleague going back to before the war, had suggested a celebration in a
Chinese restaurant where there was a band and a dance floor. Among the
party was the assistant editor, Joan Morduch. I asked her to dance, she
said yes, and we spent the rest of the evening together.

Joan had worked in the industry for ten years. From the BBC she'd
gone on to work for Alan Osbiston, the editor of *Lord Jim*, first as dub-
bing assistant and then assistant editor on *The Guns of Navarone* and *The
Victors*.

From Hong Kong the *Lord Jim* unit moved to Cambodia, where we filmed in the ruins of the twelfth-century Buddhist temple Angkor Wat, in the middle of the jungle.

I remember animals everywhere. Bats infested the ruins. A nearby lake was full of water snakes. The tiled walk outside my hotel room was inches deep in brown cockroaches, and I had to put down a strip of rubber to stop them getting under the door. A gardener was bitten by a snake. Our unit doctor, on leave from Vietnam – just a tiny war, he told us – treated him with every kind of serum till he hit the right one. Joan's Cambodian assistant invited us to a local restaurant. Flies kept falling into our food and drink, but we couldn't have cared less.

Prince Sihanouk came for the annual festival of dance. Sitting in the moonlight watching the art of the dancers set against this fantastic flood-lit background of the ancient ruins was unforgettable. Chambermaids and laundry girls by day, these shy, self-effacing people became magically transformed by their beautiful costumes and head-dresses. Joan and I often wonder what became of those gentle Cambodians in the terrible years that followed.

On our return to England Joan and I got married. After the ceremony at Kensington Registry Office, we went on to the Savoy where we celebrated with our families and old friends, including Victor and Phoebe Saville, Bill and Peggy Williams, and Anthony Asquith. After this, Joan went to Hollywood to finish editing *Lord Jim*, but she was so unhappy at our being separated that Richard Brooks let her come home.

And now Joan was about to deliver. I rushed over to the British-American Hospital to find her in premature labour. As the hours passed and nothing happened, the nurses found a bed for me in the next room. Next morning I went to the studio, leaving Joan in a state of suspended animation. Labour pains started that evening. When Joan was taken to the delivery room, I asked if I could come too.

The Spanish gynaecologist looked me up and down. 'Why not?' he said. 'Since you're here you might as well help.' He showed me the gas and oxygen cylinders. 'Be ready to give her this when I tell you.'

I followed his instructions and twenty minutes later this miracle happened before my eyes: our baby was born. I gave a shout of recognition. 'It's a boy!'

Joan managed to sit up and see our son for the first time.

We named him David. He was perfect in every way, but weighed just under three and a half pounds, so the doctors put him straight in an incubator. Every day Joan and I visited the hospital and watched him through the plate glass, naked and struggling about. Periodically the nurse came along and put her fingers through little holes in the incubator that had rubber fingers attached to them so that she could feed him. She told us it was unusual for a seven-month premature child to have such developed baby-like features.

After five weeks David graduated to a specially sterilized room, and finally Joan, suitably gowned and masked, was allowed to enter the room and make her first physical contact.

Then we were told we could take him home. On the plane we put him on the table in front of us. We ate nothing but just sat there sipping champagne and gazing at our little son. He slept through the journey and all the way to our flat in Kensington. Whether his first night at home was peaceful I don't recall, but as for his parents, suddenly having a new baby on our hands and wondering if he was all right, I don't think we slept a wink.

14 How to Burnish a Shield

After *Lawrence of Arabia*, made in the desert with real heat and dust, it made a change on *Zhivago* to go into the studio and replicate a simple substance like snow. Tricky technical problems like that come up all the time, and I always enjoyed the challenge of finding practical solutions.

I remember back in 1918 when they were shooting *First Men on the Moon*, the rocks were made of plaster, and to give the impression of zero gravity they used hidden trampolines. When the actor stepped out of the spacecraft, he landed on the first trampoline, sailed through the air, bounced off the second, and so on. This was all shot in slow motion so as to create the illusion of weightlessness.

During the 1930s the craft of film-making improved by leaps and bounds, so to speak. When Herbert Wilcox made *Victoria The Great* in 1937, royal locations were not available and we made do in the studio on a limited budget. In those days sets didn't always have ceilings, but Herbert felt they were necessary for this film to look authentic. We used two techniques common at the time: hanging miniatures and the Schufftan process.

A hanging miniature is a small-scale three-dimensional version of the real thing, hung just in front of the lens. Although it's shot in the foreground, on screen it looks like background because of perspective. Castles, mountains, etc. can appear in the distance without the unit having to go any further than the studio lot. In the case of a room, the walls are constructed normal size and the ceiling is the miniature, then the two are aligned precisely. We used this for the royal apartments.

The Schufftan process (invented by Eugene Schufftan, a German cameraman who later went to Hollywood and won an Oscar for *The Hustler*) dated from the 1920s and was available for hire. A couple of Germans, Willi and Fritz, came down to the studio and set up the apparatus. First you went to a real place – in this case the ballroom at Buckingham Palace – and took a ten-by-eight-inch still photograph of the ceiling. The photograph was then reflected by a mirror set at an angle of forty-five degrees to the lens. Looking through the lens, you see the set – the walls, floor, furniture, etc. – in the bottom half of the frame, and in the top half you have this reflected image of the ceiling. As with a hanging miniature, tracking or panning are impossible. You use it for a long shot, then cut to a medium shot in which the ceiling is outside the frame.

One of these scenes is a night shot with dozens of chandeliers in the ceiling. I took a pin and scored the photograph at the point of each candle. Backed with tracing paper this made each candle appear to be lit.

It's obviously better if these effects are planned beforehand, but often when you're in the middle of filming something unexpected arises. On *The 7th Dawn* the Bill Holden character is in the jungle trying to get back to the city, and Lewis Gilbert decided we needed some plot business to slow him down. The idea was that torrential rain would sweep away a rope bridge across a river, requiring him to make a long detour. It was decided to use a miniature.

With miniatures an essential point is to use slow motion. It is a feature of perspective that actions in the distance seem to take place much more slowly: a man passing across your line of vision takes longer to do so the further he is away. If you film four times speeded up (ninety-six frames per second instead of the usual twenty-four frames), then the miniature seems not only four times further away but also four times bigger.

This miniature was made by the art director, John Stoll. A fifteen-feet channel was dug down a slope. At the top and out of shot a big tank of water was prepared. John stuck some small branches and foliage in the foreground and some larger ones on the far side of the channel to merge with the jungle in the background. Across the channel he placed a miniature of the rope bridge. The camera rolled, the tank was tipped over, and water poured down, sweeping away the rope bridge. I admired John Stoll for improvising this – it wasn't in the script – in a matter of two or three days.

On *Caesar and Cleopatra* the difficulty was the sky. Usually a unit goes on location first, then later the art department creates sets and backgrounds to go with that footage. In this case, we had started in the studio, with exteriors shot inside against a stylized sky backing. When we went out to Egypt later, we found the real sky was different from how we'd imagined it.

The problem was to match the location sky with the studio footage.

To solve this I used a glass shot. Half a dozen plate-glass windows were bought in Cairo and mounted in frames. The scenic artist painted sky on the upper part of the glass, leaving the lower part clear. The glass was placed a few feet in front of the camera, and we shot through it at the actors beyond. On the screen the audience sees the Roman legionnaires marching across the desert beneath a fleecy blue sky. We used the glass shot not only for the sky, but also to show a pyramid or the temple of Karnak in the distance.

On *Solomon and Sheba*, filmed in Spain in 1958, the question arose: how to burnish the shields? In the Biblical story, when Solomon is fighting the Egyptians and about to be beaten, God comes to the rescue, telling Solomon to order his men to 'burnish their shields' – i.e. make them shine. Next morning the Egyptians attack with the rising sun behind them. The Israelites hold up their polished shields, reflecting the sun back into the eyes of the attacking Egyptians, who lose their sense of direction and drive their chariots over a cliff.

This was all in the script. The director, King Vidor, asked me, 'How are we going to do this, Freddie?'

I thought about this. 'We need some mirrors. Put them in frames and direct them so the sun is reflected on the camera.'

'Mirrors?' said King. 'I thought cameramen were always trying to avoid mirrors because they flare up in the lens.'

'That's exactly what we want. And it has to be mirrors because polished brass won't be anywhere near bright enough.'

The production manager said, 'That's going to cost a lot of money. We'll need at least a hundred.'

There was no other way to do it. We filmed several angles: a long shot from the point of view of the Egyptian chariots, with the camera tracking forward and the light from the mirrors flaring on the lens; a closer shot of the shields – real shields highly polished, not mirrors; more tracking shots, giving a sideways view of the charioteers reacting to the blinding.

The scene continues with the chariots plunging down a crevasse. Some of these shots were done by tilting the camera to exaggerate the slope and speeding up the film, others used models and dummies being thrown off the cliff, then at the bottom of the cliff there was a setting arranged by the special-effects man with broken wheels, some actors and some dummies.

The chariots were rented from Cecil B. de Mille, and everybody hated them. The design, taken from Egyptian friezes, was terrible. The axles were too far back, which threw all the weight forward, so when the chariot went over rough ground the poor old horse felt every bump. This had been pointed out to De Mille, but he had insisted on authenticity. In all probability the original drawings were out of proportion or deliberately stylized, since it's difficult to believe the ancient Egyptians would have failed to notice how impractical they were. We in our innocence had assumed that chariots used by De Mille, maker of *The Ten Commandments*, would be functional. Our Master of Horse, an experienced man who had worked for John Ford, was very upset by this.

By the mid-1960s virtually all films were made in colour. This wasn't always popular with film-makers, because there are some subjects that cry out to be done in black and white. In 1966 I was invited to New York by Sidney Lumet to discuss the photography for *The Deadly Affair*. He felt colour was too glamorous for a John Le Carré spy movie, but Columbia insisted. They had recently made a policy to shoot no more films in black and white, probably because it would be more difficult to sell them to TV. Sidney asked me, 'Is there anything you can do to subdue the colour and take the prettiness out of it?'

Freddie and director Sidney Lumet (centre) at work on *The Deadly Affair* (1967). James Mason is at the right corner of picture.

I returned to London pondering this, and on the Monday morning I went down to the studio and did some tests. I got a white card, illuminated it with a couple of lamps, and photographed it with reduced exposure. I tried four exposures: 30 per cent of normal, 10, 20 and 40 per cent. Then I rewound the film and photographed a few things in the studio and outside in the sunlight.

The effect was to mute the colours without changing their value. Sidney was pleased and we decided to shoot the whole film with 30 per cent pre-exposed film. Exposing the film through the camera was risky because of the danger of scratching, so we asked Technicolor to do it for us in the laboratory.

Afterwards I wrote articles for *American Cinematographer* and the BSC journal describing this technique, which I called pre-fogging. Responses from other cameramen who tried it were varied: some were quite pleased, others didn't think much of it. The most enthusiastic was Vilmos Zsigmond, who told me a few years later, 'That pre-fogging article you wrote changed my life. I've pre-fogged every film I've done since.'

Sidney Lumet had started in TV, where they love to use wide-angle lenses, perhaps because they have small sets and they like to get in close. With a wide-angle lens a close-up distorts the face. An upward angle is even worse, making the chin look huge and the forehead small. In a horror film that would be fine, but it certainly doesn't enhance an actor's beauty. I could see that Simone Signoret, a lovely person but by then no longer young, was perturbed at being photographed in this way. But then, everyone admired Lumet: if you chose to act in one of his films you had to put up with it.

Another director interested in colour experiments was John Huston, whose cameraman was Ossie Morris. On *Reflections in a Golden Eye* Ossie used a method called de-saturated colour. This too aimed at toning down the brightness, but unlike pre-fogging it was done in the lab after filming. The disadvantage, from the director's point of view, was that it gave the studio the opportunity to produce prints in normal colour if they didn't like the muted colour, whereas pre-fogging, using already doctored stock, is a *fait accompli*.

I worked with John Huston in 1968, on *Sinful Davey*. John had a highly original style of directing. He was always talking to the production manager about racing, and laying bets. I would be busy lighting and getting the set ready, then I'd say, 'All right, John, we're ready.'

Very often John had his back to the camera. 'OK. Roll 'em.'

When the shot was finished I'd say, 'Shall we cut?'

'All right, cut.'

Ossie Morris told me later, 'Oh yes, John's like that. Mad on race-horses. And sometimes not terribly interested in the film he's shooting.' But this nonchalance must have been a pose: Huston's record as a director speaks for itself.

John could be very charming. 'I need you, my dear boy,' he said when he first phoned. I told him Joan and I were about to go on holiday. 'Bring your wife. I'll give her a marvellous time.' His original camera crew had been sent to look at a location in Galway. Flying in a thick mist, they hit the top of a mountain and crashed. No one was killed, fortunately, but he needed me to take over.

Over in Ireland I visited the injured men in hospital. Ted Scaife and his operator, Ernie Day, both had broken limbs. It can be a hazardous business, working in the camera crew, when you consider some of the wild locations that have to be reached and the spectacular sequences – explosions, car crashes – that we film. It's worse for the second unit, and I suppose the most dangerous job is aerial photography. Two good friends of mine were killed in this way: Johnny Jordan and Skeets Kelly.

Johnny was injured on *You Only Live Twice*, filming from a helicopter inside the crater of Mount Shinmoe in Japan. He was leaning out to get a better angle, when a gust of wind caught one of the other helicopters and dragged it towards his. The rotor blade sliced his leg. He was rushed to hospital and after several operations they finally had to amputate, below the knee. But Johnny never lost his love of flying. On *The Battle of Britain* I offered him a job on the ground crew and he turned it down, preferring to film in the air. In 1970 he was working on *Catch 22* over the Gulf of Mexico, this time in an aeroplane. Another plane passed close, the slipstream drew him out, and he fell 2,000 feet to his death. Johnny always refused to wear a safety harness. Many people felt that if he'd been strapped in, or if he hadn't taken off his artificial leg, he might have been all right.

Skeets was killed while doing a day's work on *Zeppelin* over the Irish Sea. A few hours later the London *Evening Standard* phoned for my recollections of Skeets from the time he first worked for me, aged fifteen. It was eerie to be writing an obituary of Skeets for the second time – the first being during the war when he was shot down, presumed dead.

Skeets was a lively character and a great raconteur. On location, sitting round in the pub in the evenings, he had this great fund of stories he'd come out with. On top of the tragic fact of his death, it turned out he

wasn't insured. The producer, who was also killed in the crash, was supposed to have taken out insurance but in fact he hadn't. There was a whip-
round in the industry, but obviously it didn't match the compensation
their families should have been entitled to. The ACTT was furious and
from then on they insisted on aerial cameramen being shown the actual
insurance documents before they were allowed to go up in a plane.

Speaking for myself, I've been fairly lucky, hardly missing a day's work
from accident or illness, although I did once fall off a car.

Car sequences used to be done with back projection. The invention of
the low loader changed all that. The actors' car is placed on this low-slung
trailer pulled by the camera truck; on screen it looks as if the car is driving
on the road. The operator can work from the camera truck, or squat with
hand-held camera on the bumper or bonnet of the car, or he can get inside
the car and shoot from the front passenger seat or the rear. Or the camera
can be fixed on the outside of the car to film in through the window. And
sometimes you dispense with the low loader and have the actor drive the
car, though you try to avoid this, for safety reasons.

Shortly after my eightieth birthday I was working on *Invitation to the
Wedding*, filming on a Rolls-Royce. My operator Chic Anstiss was
crouched in the front seat, shooting three actors sitting in the back. I was
standing on the running-board outside, hanging on to the window, so I
could watch what was going on inside. At the end of the shot the driver
turned round on a grass verge. It happened that we were on a slight slope,
enough to make me lose my grip. I was thrown off and landed flat on my
back in the grass. My head went thump – if it had been concrete I'd have
split it open. Everyone dashed towards me, afraid I'd been hurt. I just got
up and said, 'I'm OK.' I was a bit shaken but I didn't let on.

Transport to and from locations can be hazardous. On *You Only Live
Twice* we filmed in a mountainous region of the southern island of Japan.
The rim of the extinct volcano of Mount Shinmoe was wide enough only
for a two-seater helicopter, and many of the crew had to go up on horseback then on foot, slogging it through the mud. We had just got the last
shot in the can when a thick mist descended, making flying impossible.
We had to carry all the equipment, scrambling the two miles down to the
plateau where the horses were waiting.

Like other James Bond movies, *You Only Live Twice* combined story
and action with local colour. In Kyoto we filmed in a traditional garden
with sandy paths threading harmoniously between formal fish-ponds,
wooden bridges and ornamental rest-houses. The gardener found the

presence of a film unit a bit hard to take. Every time we walked on a path he would follow us, raking over our footprints.

I found the customs of Japan fascinating. One sequence featured sumo wrestling. These huge, fat wrestlers with elaborate hair styles come on and throw salt on the earth-packed floor. They circle each other and grapple. A moment later one is thrown and it's all over. In our bare hotel rooms little girls knelt to serve us tea while we squatted cross-legged on the floor. They had public baths outside, several ones with different flavours of water: pineapple, hot sand, mud, etc.

The scriptwriter on the film was Roald Dahl, whose wife, Patricia Neal, was recovering from a bad stroke. Every morning Pat would say, 'Now I know your names. It's . . . er . . . don't tell me . . . I know you're the cameraman, and you have a little boy . . .' She had all the salient facts but not the names. It was very moving to see her struggling to get over her disability and rebuild her acting career.

Back in England Cubby Broccoli and Harry Saltzman, the producers of *You Only Live Twice*, arranged a party with over 200 guests to celebrate my fifty years in the industry, from 1917 to 1967. My old friend Anthony Asquith climbed on a table to make a speech. As President of the ACTT, he presented me with an honorary membership card. It gave me a peculiar satisfaction to think that was one subscription I wouldn't have to worry about any more!

A few months later Anthony was ill with cancer. When Joan and I went to see him in hospital, he was sitting up in bed, papers strewn all around him, writing. 'I'm much better,' he said. 'I'll be out of here by the end of the week.' And he was too: he died two days later.

Anthony was called Puff because as a child he reminded his mother of a puffin. When we were younger, he'd often come to stay for the weekend. The children loved him. He was Barbara's godfather and later, when there was thought of sending Michael to Winchester, he took us down there and introduced us to the headmaster. He would play *Monopoly* with them for hours on end, changing the rules to make it more difficult and amusing. Puff was a great talker. He used to pace up and down airing his views on every subject under the sun, then suddenly sit down and apologize for monopolizing the conversation. As a director he was just as kind and considerate to everyone. In 1947 when we worked together on *The Winslow Boy* he would say to an actor, 'I'm terribly sorry, would you *mind,* darling, emphasizing the word just a *little* more', while twisting his legs round each other and making intense contortions with his

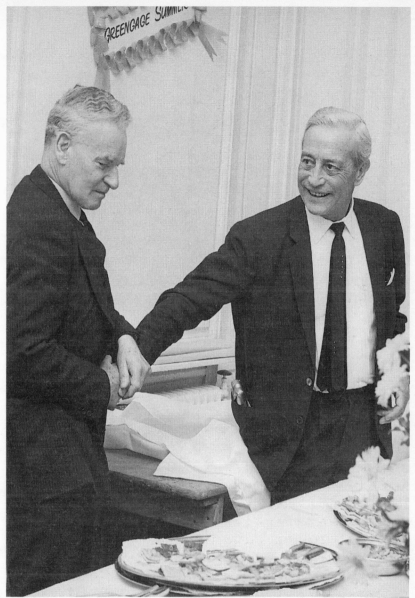

Freddie with his dear friend Anthony 'Puff' Asquith, at a party marking
Freddie's fiftieth year in films.

On location for *The Battle of Britain* (1968): Freddie poses with Sir Douglas Bader.

arms. Poor old Puff, he was a brilliant man and highly sensitive.

At the end of *You Only Live Twice* Cubby Broccoli asked me to go to Hollywood to supervise the colour grading of 600 prints required for crash release. The matrices (colour dupes) were sent out from Technicolor England reel by reel, and I reviewed and passed the prints. Cubby booked us into a sumptuous suite at the Beverly Wiltshire Hotel and arranged for Joan and me to be entertained every night and taken to baseball games, Disneyland, and so on. At the age of twenty months our son David took this in his stride, but for me it was the product of fifty years' hard slog to receive this VIP treatment.

You Only Live Twice was completed at Pinewood on a million-dollar set, designed by Ken Adam, that was the size of two football fields and took practically every lamp in the studio to light. *The Battle of Britain*, made the following year, was another large-scale project.

The producers set out to make a record of those days in the summer of 1940 when the Luftwaffe tried to draw out and then destroy the Royal Air Force. Ginger Lacey, the most decorated pilot of the war, was our permanent adviser, and we were also visited by Bob Stanford-Tuck and Douglas Bader. The film aimed to vindicate the reputation of Lord

Dowding, the head of Fighter Command, whose strategy, much criticized by his colleagues at the time, was now known to have been correct. When he came down, those old war heroes quarrelled for the honour of pushing his wheelchair, they venerated him so much. He had recently had his eyesight restored after a cataract operation, and was obviously delighted at seeing the actual Spitfires and Hurricanes that had taken part in the battle. Laurence Olivier, who portrayed him, was proud to meet Dowding and have the opportunity to probe into the heart and soul of the man himself.

There were also some German aces, including Adolf Galland, the most decorated pilot in his country. I noticed a comradeship between the British and German airmen, both brave men fighting for their countries.

We started filming in Seville, for the simple reason that the planes were there. The Spanish Air Force had a number of Messerschmidts, used for training purposes, so the scenes supposedly in France and Germany were done in Spain, with San Sebastián standing in for the streets of Berlin and the beaches and harbour of Dunkirk. When we staged an air raid, the local authority helpfully arranged a power blackout, which affected the whole town. It's difficult to imagine that happening in England.

The actual Battle of Britain was fought during a period of glorious sunshine, but the summer of 1968 in England was wet and miserable. In some films you can adapt the story and make do with bad weather, but in this case it would have been impossible. You can't film aerial combats if the sky is overcast. What's more, it would have been historically inaccurate. They didn't fly in bad weather in 1940. Without radar they would have run the risk of crashing into one another.

So much time was lost that we started playing games of football, just for something to do. Once Joan brought little David along, telling him they were going to watch me at work. When he saw me, he put two and two together, and asked, 'Is Daddy a footballer?'

At Duxford there was an old hangar, which we were given permission to blow up. There is a technique for doing these things. The special-effects people rig up a wood and plaster set that is deliberately flimsy, with the timbers half sawn through. They drill holes at strategic places, put dynamite in them, and wire all the charges to one switch beside the camera. When the switch is pulled the whole thing is blown apart, collapses and bursts into flames.

That's what happens with a set, which has been constructed specially to be knocked down. With a real, solid building it's not quite so simple.

The scene called for Susannah York and Kenneth More to be standing in the airfield, talking, with the hangar in the background. Suddenly an enemy plane comes over, strafing and bombing. They run – towards the camera – and dive for cover into the nearest trench. At that point the director was to make a signal, someone would pull the switch, and BOOM!

We ran the camera and let rip. The result was not quite what we had in mind. There was a dull thud, the hangar shook slightly, and remained standing. A tense couple of minutes followed before Cliff Richardson and his special-effects team dared venture into the building. They attached some more sticks of dynamite and we tried again. The second time it went a bit better, but it was still disappointing. The hangar came down, but not in the spectacular way I'd hoped.

While the main unit struggled through the long, cold summer photographing the dramatic scenes, there were other units doing the aerial stuff. They had a specially converted B-25 bomber with four internal camera positions and an apparatus on a retracting double-jointed arm that could be lowered to give the operator a 360-degree sweep. They also used helicopters, which accompanied the Spitfires and Hurricanes flying into battle. At the same time there was yet another unit shooting radio-controlled models against the sky. Finally we went to Pinewood to weld all the flying material together. This involved weeks of painstaking effort, using front and back projection, matte process and other techniques.

In front projection the projector and the camera are locked together next to each other, pointing at a huge sixty feet by forty feet screen fifty yards away, with a prism on the camera so that the alignment on the screen is identical for both. Live actors or models are photographed in the foreground against this screen on which is projected background material filmed previously. In this case the background was sky, clouds, German planes, and in the foreground we had, hanging on thin nylon cords, a line of miniature Spitfires. The largest, a few feet long, were nearest the camera; the smallest, a few inches long, were further away. This gave the perspective of aeroplanes in flight apparently up to a mile in the distance.

The older technique of back projection has the projector on the far side of the screen. With front projection you get a more exact alignment between the two images and therefore better definition. Also, because of the highly reflective quality of the front-projection screen you have more light, better exposure, sharper focus. Against these advantages you have to set the fact that front projection is complicated to set up and costs much more. On a brief sequence it's often not worth the trouble of using it.

For every special-effects shot there's always one method that stands out as the right one. It may be matte process – when you shoot actors against a blue screen, the scenic artist paints a background and the two images are printed together in the lab – or the simplest technique of all: the painted backcloth. In the *Battle of Britain* dogfights, when a plane is hit you want a three-second cut to a close-up of the pilot in his blazing cockpit. For this shot the scenic artist painted a six by eight feet piece of canvas as blue sky with some cloud to match up with the long shot, and we filmed a dummy cockpit against this backing. At Pinewood they have different specialists for all these methods.

Working on *The Battle of Britain* was an interesting experience, but on the whole I don't much care for the trick stuff. I prefer actors and getting on with the story. Around this time I received a letter from David Lean. His new film would be made entirely on location on the west coast of Ireland. Would I 'do battle' with him again? I cabled back two words: 'Yes, please!'

David Lean and co., fighting the unruly elements on *Ryan's Daughter* (1970).

Before we started the film David sent me another letter, twenty-two pages long. He praised some of my ideas – the mirage shot, Lara's hand, the vignette of Zhivago – and said that on *Ryan's Daughter* he hoped to go further, to get away from 'the fetish of realism', and to use the camera expressively rather than naturalistically. He also wanted me as cameraman to participate fully in the picture, rather than be someone just hired to do a job, as cameramen are usually made to feel.

In January 1969 Joan and I went to Ireland to look at the location. David had scouted the whole of the west coast before choosing the Dingle peninsula in County Kerry, four hours' drive from Dublin. The setting was a bleak hillside battered by winds whipping in from the Atlantic and surrounded by mountains on three sides. It was grim and spectacular.

Here they built the 1916 set, designed by Stephen Grimes. It was a whole village, including shops, a schoolhouse, church, pub and a post office. Most sets are just facades, made of plaster and hardboard, but for this film they used real stone. Anything less substantial would never have stood up to the gales. Two hundred workmen built the houses, using slate and 20,000 tons of granite from a dozen local quarries. Many had fitted interiors, with ceilings, lighting, plumbing and working fire grates. When finished, 'Kirrary' became the westernmost village in the European land mass – though not for long, because at the end of filming the whole thing had to be torn down and the land returned to the farmers in its original condition.

The shooting schedule was supposed to be five months – it ended up much longer – so Joan and I rented a seaside 'chalet' for ourselves and David, then aged three. The nearest hamlet was called Ballydavid; we felt the name was a good omen.

Back in England I picked the crew and ordered cameras, generators and lighting equipment. This is always a ticklish business because there are so many imponderables, such as the weather, schedule changes, actors' contractual dates. One must allow for the maximum requirements, because in a remote location like this if you suddenly find yourself short of a brute, say, you're stuck. I also bought some protective clothing for the storms we planned to film.

Shooting started in mid February. The evening before, my chief gaffer Bernie Prentice turned up at the chalet with his electricians and escorted me down to the local pub where all fourteen of them insisted on buying me a drink. When they took me home I found Bob Huke, the second-unit cameraman, had dropped by to confer over dinner. I don't think our discussion can have been very productive.

The first thing we noticed was the changing light conditions. One moment we would be enveloped in a mist so thick it was impossible to see the end of the street, the next it would miraculously disperse, disclosing a glorious view of the distant hills and ocean. This made continuity very difficult in the exterior sequences, whilst indoors one had to constantly adjust the lighting to balance the differing qualities of daylight coming in through the windows.

Because of the erratic weather the shooting schedule had to be flexible. As winter gave way to spring, we alternated shooting from the village street to the schoolhouse to the beaches. When the weather was suitable we filmed outdoors; when it wasn't we moved inside and shot scenes in the pub or the schoolmaster's house.

Ryan's Daughter: a freshly bearded Freddie presides over the massed ranks of light.

The ceilings were very low, which made overhead lighting almost impossible. The pub had been constructed with removable panels so that lamps could be squeezed in between the rafters, provided they were out of shot. Otherwise, we had to light from the floor and through the windows. It got very cramped in those buildings. David Lean had insisted on using Panavision 70-mm cameras, which needed more light than 35-mm and hence more equipment. You can imagine the difficulty of making space for a camera crew of four, the sound men, the director, continuity, electricians, not to mention the actors. Despite these difficulties, I think having sets like that was worth it, because watching the film you really do get the feeling you're within four walls.

On the beach the tide sometimes came in awfully fast. Once David got his teeth into a scene you didn't want to call a halt, and we would often be shooting with the sea washing round our ankles. Then we would have to rescue the camera and ourselves, with a long, arduous scramble up the rocks to safety. The only vehicle that could traverse the beach when it was covered with water was the caterpillar tractor, and this saved us more than once. What with the wind and spray, the sensitive cameras always had to be shielded against the salty air. One morning, waking up to find blood on my pillow, I realized I'd have to give up shaving. The last time I'd grown a beard was in Hudson Bay on *49th Parallel* thirty years before.

Ryan's Daughter: Freddie walks a line in the sand for Sarah Miles's instruction.

In the beach scenes the character of Ryan's daughter, played by Sarah
Miles, often carries a parasol, symbolizing her wayward aspirations. In
one scene a gust of wind blows the parasol out of her hands and over the
cliff. That may sound simple, but it took us four or five hours to get it
right. We had a track built on the cliff top pointing out to sea, and a wind
machine standing by to make sure the parasol blew in the right direction.
When the parasol left her, we tracked it right to the edge of the cliff then
panned downwards, following its path. Everyone had lifelines round
them, but it was still scary.

One of the most memorable sequences in *Ryan's Daughter* is the
storm. There are special difficulties in filming storms. When you shoot in
the rain you have a cover, sometimes a big umbrella, over the camera to
keep water off the lens, and even then you still get the odd drip. In a
strong wind the rain drives straight at the lens and just blurs everything
out. This is why storms are normally done in a studio tank with models
lashed by aeroplane propellers. On *Lord Jim*, for instance, the shipwreck
sequence was shot on a large stage flooded to a depth of four feet, and we
spent several days in wet suits, surrounded by artificial fog. I always
thought there must be a better way of doing it.

On the bridge of ships they have a piece of glass attached to the outside
of the window. This spins very fast, and any spray is shaken off by cen-
trifugal force. It seemed to me this idea could be adapted for use as a kind
of lens cap on a camera. We tried it out, and it worked perfectly. This is
what enabled us to shoot an actual storm in *Ryan's Daughter*. The device
is called Clear Screen and can be hired from Samuelsons'.

At first the storm sequence was shot on a beach near Dingle, with fire
hoses and wind machines directed at the actors. After seeing the rushes,
David decided this footage was a bit tame, and we would shoot in a real
force nine. Whenever we received advance warning of an approaching
storm, the unit would make a two-hour journey to the more exposed
rocky coast of the Ennis Peninsula.

Here we'd get the full fury of the Atlantic Ocean with nothing between
us and America to break the violence of the storm. The cameras had to be
literally chained to the rocks and the actors were on safety ropes, but it
was still dangerous. John Mills nearly drowned when his boat capsized.
For his village idiot character John had a set of false teeth. When he realized he was going to be thrown in the water, John had the presence of
mind to take out the teeth and slip them in his pocket so they weren't lost,
much to the make-up man's relief.

The storm might continue for an hour then clear up, so we'd go back and get on with some other part of the story and wait for the next storm warning, which might not come for several days. In the finished film the sequence lasts about ten minutes, but to get this footage took several months of intermittent work. When winter came and we hadn't completed the summer scenes, the main unit moved to South Africa, leaving a second unit headed by Roy Stevens, with Denys Coop in charge of the photography. At one point Roy was knocked over by a wave and suffered severe concussion and bruising, but he managed to complete the sequence. The result is to my mind the most realistic storm ever shown on the screen.

The rushes were viewed in a church hall with our own projector. One day David, who had what I can only call acute vision, declared that the rushes were not very sharp – in other words, out of focus. After a somewhat stormy session it was decided to take another look using superior projection facilities. A strange and apprehensive party of us journeyed to Dublin, and somewhere about midnight we viewed our rushes on what was considered the best screen in the city. David was still dissatisfied with the focus. Back in the hotel we argued about it over numerous cups of coffee until 4 o'clock in the morning. Next day we examined the footage in yet another cinema. To my intense relief the projection was pinpoint sharp. All of us – Bob Huke, Norman Savage, my operator Ernie Day and myself – agreed on this. We informed David of our finding. He still didn't believe me, but after a further look back in Dingle he turned abruptly to me and said, 'It's bloody sharp.'

I just nodded and that was the end of the episode. Viewing rushes, when you see before you the product of some very hard labour, is always a tense business. Even so, I have to rate this the most miserable two days of our stay in Ireland.

MGM always liked to have some well-known American star in a film for box-office appeal in the States, so they cast Robert Mitchum, who was excellent, and Christopher Jones. Christopher had made his name in a film called *Three in the Attic*, and MGM thought they had a find, a new James Dean. This long-haired, pale-faced, sad-looking actor joined us, and over a period of several days and tests we gradually chopped his hair off till it got down to a reasonable length for a British Army captain in the 1914–18 war.

Then we discovered Christopher was practically inarticulate.

In an early scene he's with a major leaving for the front who admits to the Jones character his fear at this prospect. At the beginning of the scene Christopher had some lines to say. David rehearsed the actors, then he said, 'All right, let's try it. Action.'

The camera started turning and Christopher sat there. He didn't say anything, or do anything, but just stared ahead. David said 'Cut', and spoke to Christopher, who made no response. Finally David exclaimed, 'For Christ's sake, Christopher, what's the matter with you?'

'I'm not an actor,' he replied.

There was a stony silence. We all wondered what we were going to do, with a leading man on our hands who couldn't act.

David took me aside and said, 'Throw him in silhouette as much as you can.' I made his face dark, with a little slit across the eyes. David played the scene with the camera mainly on the other actor, Gerald Sim. Christopher was just sitting there trembling, but you'd probably think he was good too, with the lighting and the other fellow pacing up and down doing all the work.

Throughout the film we had to deal with Christopher in certain tricky little ways like this to cover up the woodenness of his acting. Later, during editing, it was decided to use another actor, Julian Holloway, to overdub his voice. If a director is committed to a player whom he suddenly realizes isn't any good, then he avoids shooting on him, concentrating on another actor who is. This is how David solved the problem of Christopher. What you see of him is what you were intended to see, but it doesn't show you how difficult it was to get it.

Ryan's Daughter is about the senses, David told me at the beginning. At certain points the mood was to be light and fresh, at others ominous and heavy. Whenever possible we used the weather – the storm, for instance – to our advantage, but the elements didn't always provide the atmosphere we were looking for and we had to create it ourselves. In one scene Sarah Miles gets up in the early morning, leaving her husband in bed, and meets her lover out in the garden. Behind them we see looming clouds. As it happened, on the day of shooting the sky was bright and sunny, and the illusion of dark clouds was created by burning motor tyres just off camera.

In another scene Robert Mitchum kneels by the grave of his first wife, and the sole of his upturned boot is seen in close-up. The film then cuts to Sarah Miles walking along the beach. She comes to his boot prints in the sand, puts her bare foot in one, then another, following the tracks he's made. Before filming we polished the hobnail pattern in the sole bright so the audience would pick up on it and make the connection.

Up in the air on *Ryan's Daughter*: Freddie and David Lean ride the crane . . .

. . . for the benefit of a shot with saddlebound Sarah Miles.

It's only by taking infinite care over details like this that you make memorable pictures.

Meanwhile we were all making ourselves at home on this windswept peninsula. I remember a lot of parties and socializing. The property department made a slide and swing set for David and the other children in the unit. We planted a passable vegetable and flower garden, and tried to grow sweet peas. There were no trees or hedges locally, only stone walls, so we had to drive the forty miles to Tralee to buy some canes. Practically every night I'd arrive home to find the canes flattened by the gales, and I tied more and more pieces of string to rocks to strengthen the support. It became a constant battle with the elements, a small-scale version of our daily struggle shooting on the beach.

There was a local elderly couple, the Grummels, to help us out with domestic chores, and I had Mr Grummel build us a hen run. Our four hens gave us three or four eggs a day, and on St Patrick's Day they came up trumps with a record five. One morning I went out to feed the hens and one of them was dead. I took it away in the car and brought back a similar one in the evening so my son wouldn't notice.

Ryan's Daughter was all made on location as David Lean was keen to avoid the artificiality that comes with even the best studio conditions, but in the end he had to compromise. We had run wildly over schedule. It was now December and raining almost every day, and we still had to do the scene where Sarah Miles and the captain go into the woods and make love. We managed to get some shots: one of a haze of bluebells through the trees, which David had spotted earlier in the year and thought would look effective, another of Chris and Sarah riding through a spot of sunlight in the trees, and a closer shot of them dismounting. Then, at the point where he takes her into his arms, it started to rain and we packed up for the day.

David particularly wanted this scene to be warm and sunny, because they make love in the woods on the ground, which of course you can hardly do in the rain. So in desperation we decided to film the scene indoors.

I had done this sort of thing many times before. I remember on *Ivanhoe* the director, Richard Thorpe, got fed up with the English climate. We were shooting the climax of the film – a duel with swords and maces in the jousting fields of Ashby-de-la-Zouch – out on the studio lot. Every time we got going it poured with rain, the cast were soaked and the costumes had to be dried out and ironed. Finally Richard said, 'Hell, this is no good. Let's put it all in the studio.' The art department painted a sky-back all the way round the stage. They reduced the width of the tents, put up two feet of peat on the floor, and we shot the rest of the scene in there. Provided you obey the cardinal rule – light the set to avoid multiple shadows – you can get away with it.

And that's how we filmed the love scene in *Ryan's Daughter*. We used the village dance hall, turning it into a makeshift studio. The art director put a cyclorama round the back for the sky, and Eddie Fowlie and his assistants brought in truckloads of trees and turf. They also created a little pond with a plastic bottom. We had quite a few arc lamps in there, and although it was December it became hot and humid in this little hut. Within a few days the foliage was quite luxuriant, birds came in and were flying around the set. As a final symbolic touch, Eddie had kept some dandelion heads, and at the climactic moment the seeds were gently wafted across the actors.

We shot the rest of the love scene in there, which undoubtedly was more comfortable for the actors than the sopping wet woods of Killarney, where the scene had been started. At the time we thought the love-making daring, but by today's standards it would be considered merely charming. I'm sure no one seeing the film would realize this sequence was done indoors. The point is, when faking becomes unavoidable, if it is done well the audience won't notice.

After that we gave up shooting in Dingle. The decision was made to complete the summer scenes in South Africa. The changeover would take a few weeks, and David suggested that Joan and I travelled by sea. This would enable me to rest my back, which I had strained foolishly trying to lift a lamp instead of waiting for the electricians to do it.

We stayed in South Africa for about five weeks, filming on the beaches near Cape Town. The white rocks had to be sprayed black to resemble those in Ireland, and as we were closer to the equator, the sun was higher in the sky, which meant adjusting the facial lighting accordingly. On one of the beaches we came across an old wreck, which David decided to incorporate into the last scene of the film, when the captain blows himself into oblivion. This action was meant to coincide with the sun sinking into the ocean, but a bank of clouds kept appearing on the horizon just before sunset, ruining the effect we were after and extending the schedule yet again. Finally it was all wrapped up and we returned to England again by sea.

In the meanwhile David Lean had moved his headquarters to the Great Southern Hotel in Killarney, where he was busy editing the picture. He now asked me to join him with a skeleton camera crew to film the title background.

We were asked to shoot 250 feet, which was the length of the credits. It was a dawn sequence, which on the screen would be speeded up, so in filming it we turned the camera one frame every minute. This is called time-lapse photography. We arranged the set-up in advance, aligning the camera to avoid telegraph poles, making marks on the ground that we'd be able to find in the dark, and asking the farmer to remove his sheep which otherwise would appear to be darting about all over the field. Next morning we were up before dawn to be ready to shoot. The effect was interesting. The screen starts off completely black, then it gets lighter and you gradually see the shape of the valley and the clouds, which are going by very fast, as in a great storm, and finally the sun comes up.

Not long before we left Joan and I celebrated our wedding anniversary by giving a small dinner party. In the middle there was a phone call from my daughter Barbara, telling me I had been awarded the OBE in the Queen's Birthday Honours.

When the film came out, MGM asked me to go on a lecture tour of America. Mostly it's actors who do these promotions, but the company decided there was now an interest in the technical side of films. At first I was petrified, but I soon started to enjoy myself. It was quite tough going: television or radio early in the morning, press interviews over lunch, and evening lectures at museums and colleges. Excerpts were shown from *Doctor Zhivago* and *Ryan's Daughter*, then the audience would ask how we managed to produce certain effects. At one venue, Sheridan College in Toronto, the students asked me to light a film they were making of my lecture. My last lecture was at MGM's Culver City, and I was sad to see that most of the stages were idle and there was a general atmosphere of dejection and uncertainty.

I loved *Ryan's Daughter*. While we were filming, taking months and months over it, the industry was at a low ebb and those out of work were grumbling that all that money could have been spread over two or three pictures. I can't agree with this view. I remember one shot of Sarah Miles amidst a shimmering stretch of sandy beach and waves. Any other director might have wanted her in a big close-up, but David Lean was thinking, I suppose, of the loneliness of the landscape and within it this tiny figure walking along with her sunshade. To produce a narrative of such sweep, with such richness of detail, you just have to spend a lot of money. David's films have been hugely popular, and for the three Oscars I have won photographing them I can only thank David for the opportunity.

16 Freddie's a Tough Man

When I worked with David Lean he once remarked, 'Freddie, you're the hardest-working cameraman I ever worked with.' I suppose it comes down to whether you're prepared to put in the extra mile. When you get back to the hotel after twelve hours' shooting in some god-forsaken spot, you don't always feel like driving out to take a look at another location, or sitting around till the small hours discussing the next day's work. Some cameramen might say, 'I'm whacked. I think I'll just have a couple of beers and turn in.' And they might be right. One can push oneself too far.

I've always been blessed with a lot of energy. But it's also a question of attitude. The way I see it, there's a lot more to being a cameraman than lighting the set and supervising the operating of the camera. On a film you have carpenters, painters, plasterers, electricians, property men, stage-hands, hairdressers, make-up people. The cameraman has something to do with all these people because everything is seen through the eye of the lens. If you find something's not up to standard, you have to get the person who's responsible for it and have it put right.

It's been my lot to be abrasive. I pride myself that at British and Dominions in the 1930s and MGM in the 1950s I created camera departments that were regarded as the most efficient in England. To do that I often had to get tough with men who weren't pulling their weight. There used to be a lot of lazy people in the film industry. I'd be lighting, and I'd look up on the rail and one of the electricians would be reading a newspaper. 'Come on, Jack, snap out of it!' I'd have to say. 'Turn that lamp over here.' It was my job to light the set, and if I didn't get co-operation from an electrician I'd have to bawl him out.

By the 1960s attitudes had changed. People were much more professional. Out in Jordan on *Lawrence* a new electrician was sent to replace someone who'd become ill because of the heat. A few days later I happened to be having a drink with this newcomer. 'You've mellowed, Freddie,' he said. 'You're so nice now. You used to be a bit of a bastard.'

'It's not me that's changed,' I told him. 'It's you blokes. If you were a lazy sod I had to be an old bastard. It was the only way to get things done.'

But there are still occasions when a film needs a cameraman who's 'a bit of a bastard' – someone prepared to push to get things done.

The Blue Bird was made in 1975. It was the brainchild of Armand Hammer, an American millionaire and philanthropist who had built hotels and done a lot of other business in the Soviet Union. To try and improve relations between the two countries, he had the idea of a movie co-production. Maeterlinck's story was chosen. It had always been a big favourite in Russia, and was known in the United States through the 1940 film with Shirley Temple, and a harmless fairy story was thought appropriate. Twentieth Century Fox agreed to back this, and a Western cast came out to Leningrad with an American director, George Cukor, to work with the Russian crew.

And then they ran into trouble. George had had a long and versatile career tackling all kinds of subjects for MGM and other companies, but even so I don't think a fairy story was really his cup of tea. Also, the cameraman was rather inexperienced – I don't think he'd shot a colour film before. This was a great disadvantage for George, because he always relies on his cameraman to handle the photographic side while he himself concentrates on the acting and the story. As it was, the cameraman spoke no English and George no Russian, so there was no rapport between them.

After three months everyone was disappointed with the results, and they finally realized they had to do something about it. George and I had worked together twice before and he asked for me. Fox knew my reputation and supported this. It was a great loss of face for the Russians to have their man replaced, but finally they agreed that I should be asked to come and take over the photography.

I got some idea of the atmosphere awaiting me when I went to the Soviet Embassy in Kensington. The officials were cagey and unsmiling. They were obviously expecting me, and after a short interview they said, 'We'll give you a visa, but not your wife.'

'In that case,' I replied, 'I'm not going. You can have this visa back. Goodbye.'

They quickly changed their minds and produced visas for Joan and David, and we left the next day.

The first day in the studio George and I viewed the rushes of the three months' work. We decided to reshoot the whole lot. That evening at dinner George put me between Ava Gardner and Elizabeth Taylor and said, 'From now on Freddie's in charge. I'm giving up all responsibility.'

The Blue Bird (1975): on location in Leningrad, Freddie in conference with Elizabeth Taylor.

'Thanks very much,' I said sardonically, knowing he meant it.

Ava and Elizabeth seemed glad I had arrived. I'd worked with both of them before, at MGM and afterwards; in fact, this was my sixth film with Ava and my fourth with Elizabeth.

I'd insisted on bringing a Panavision camera and also my own crew: Freddie Cooper, Trevor Coop and Alan Annand. The Russian cameraman stayed on and operated the second camera from time to time. He was a bit sour at first, but after a few days he got used to it and we became the best of friends. The focus puller also remained in the unit, even though quite a lot of her work so far had been out of focus. In the Soviet Union, apparently, inefficient people were not given the sack but simply moved to a position where they could do less damage.

Filming in the Soviet Union was quite a battle because although the Russians were personally very nice, their method of work was quite different from ours. They did things at a much slower pace, and they insisted on a five-day week. This sort of thing doesn't work with film-making. You've got to crack away and when necessary do a bit of overtime. American companies always wanted to work six days, and finally the Russians were persuaded to accept this. On Saturdays it wasn't the usual crew but a lot of old men and young girls who didn't really understand what was required of them. The studio was empty except for our stage, so if we needed anything from the prop room, say, it was just too bad. Saturday was always a rotten day's work.

The lighting equipment consisted of old searchlights they'd brought back from the UFA studio in Germany at the end of the Second World War. They were enormous things with parabolic mirrors, and when you used them you got a big black hole in the middle of the illuminated area from the shadow of the carbons in the mirror. They called them brutes, but they weren't what we considered brutes. I pointed out to the producer that they were useless, and after a few weeks' delay I managed to get some real brutes and other lamps sent out from England.

The sets were solid hardwood and built to last fifty years. The spot rails were six feet wide and overlapped the set – that was their idea of a safe rail. If I wanted a lamp moved from one spot rail to another, there was a terrific palaver. 'You can't do that,' they'd say. 'You'll have to send for the committee member.'

After a quarter of an hour this large and formidable lady would come down. 'Why do you want to move the lamp?' I was asked through an interpreter.

'It's nothing to do with you,' I snapped back. 'I want to move the lamp. And I want it moved now – quick!'

A bit of shouting and bullying followed, and she walked away in disgust. They moved the lamp but it took them half an hour to get round to it. The delays on the film were appalling.

The assistant art director was a lovely girl always beautifully dressed. I asked her where she got her clothes and she explained friends sent the material from Finland. Early on in the film I spoke to her about the drapes on the set, which I thought were badly hung. She told me nothing could be done about this. I said, 'Something's got to be done because it's just not good enough.'

Overhearing this, George Cukor added, 'You do exactly what Mr Young wants.'

The girl burst into tears. I thought this incident not very helpful, so I bought a bottle of export vodka at the foreign currency shop at the hotel, and next day gave it to her. At lunch-time she beckoned me into a little art room at the back of the set. There was a group of about six – my operator, the focus puller, the art director, the props man. She poured little glasses of vodka, and we all drank a toast in the traditional manner, knocking it back in one. Then she produced another bottle, this time the regular Russian stuff, the colour of brown tea, and we finished this off too. We went off to lunch feeling very happy, and for the rest of the picture she was as friendly as could be, her whole attitude changed.

At the end of filming she and a couple of other Russians came to the airport to see us off. I was touched to notice tears in their eyes. They were obviously sorry to see us go.

One of these was Oleg Danilov, the production manager, who had been kind and helpful to us all through. After our departure the KGB rounded up the Russian crew and interrogated them about what we'd said. Oleg was so disgusted at this that he resigned his job and resolved to defect. He got a job as a seaman, jumped ship in Italy and was granted political asylum. He wrote to me, and also to several other people – George, Peter Beale of Fox, John Palmer, the production manager – asking for help and money to get to Hollywood. Eventually Fox got him a job in a film laboratory in Hollywood. He always hoped to get back into production, but the last I heard of him he was working as a taxi driver.

One of the Russians in the unit was a quiet, serious-looking chap whose job was something to do with control of money. In the studio he only spoke Russian, but one day on location he suddenly addressed us in

English. We thought he must be KGB. At one point I got frustrated at my hotel room window, which had been stuck for days. I said loudly, 'Listen, if this room is bugged, I'm trying to get my bloody window open. For Christ's sake, do something about it.' It was fixed the following day.

Our Russian colleagues loved their children, they loved their old parents, but they told me some of them were living eight or ten families to one building with one toilet. The roads of Leningrad were full of potholes, with old trams shaking through the streets and very few cars, but all the bosses had chauffeur-driven limousines.

The Russians really cared about their museums. Our chief interpreter took us to the Summer Palace at Tsarskoe Selo. It had been blown to bits in the war, and since then the painted ceilings, inlaid floors, and the domes with their gold leaf had been painstakingly restored. Inside there were enlargements on the wall showing how it had been done. In places like this and the Hermitage, you could see the beautiful workmanship, the pride in their heritage. The best things they had on show were those left over from the Tsarist regime: the museums, ballet, opera, theatre.

Visitors to the Soviet Union always complain about the food. My solution was to have parcels sent out from Fortnum and Mason. We also bought fresh food from the market, but that was a hit-and-miss-affair. One day there'd be a glut of bananas and not much else. Another day it would be melons. However, when you could get them the vegetables in season were superb. I got hold of a couple of electric burners so that I could cook these things in my hotel room.

There were many official banquets and private parties. For David, then aged nine, it was more fun than most pictures because the cast included two children of his own age, Patsy Kensit and Todd Lookinland. Joan and I gave dinner parties now and then, inviting the camera crew to share our feasts. Liz Taylor had a deep-freeze for the Mexican food she was crazy about. When her part finished and she returned to the States, we opened the freezer and found it stacked to the brim with tortillas and beans. The crew shared it out between them.

Most of the film was shot in the studio but we did one location, near Riga in Latvia. During the one-hour flight it rained and water dripped through the roof onto our heads. I'd never been in a plane that leaked before. In Riga there were more goods in the shops and an atmosphere of relative freedom. They even had a funfair on the beach. The location was in a forest where they'd taken old cottages from various parts of the Soviet Union and rebuilt them as a kind of living museum of folk crafts.

There was a set of stocks, and people carrying out the old occupations, like using a spinning-wheel. These picturesque activities made it ideal for one of the scenes in the fairy story.

At last, after five months, the picture was completed. On the whole, once we settled down, the atmosphere between ourselves and the Russians was quite friendly, though it didn't help when Western journalists came out for two or three days and wrote articles about the lousy food and having to queue up for the lift all the time. *The Blue Bird* was dubbed into about thirty languages for showing in all the republics of the Soviet Union. In the West it had hardly any distribution at all.

A few years later George Cukor gave a lecture at the National Film Theatre, and a question came up about *The Blue Bird*. George said, 'You should ask Freddie Young. Is he here?' Joan and I were there sitting near the back of the auditorium, unknown to George. I called out, 'Yes, George, I'm here.' George made some complimentary remarks about me, which was a bit embarrassing, and I got a round of applause. Afterwards we joined him for a drink on the terrace. 'Freddie's a very tough man,' George told the others. 'God knows what I would have done without him. He told them. Freddie wanted things done. They had to do it.'

He was speaking the absolute truth. That's what I was there for; not just for my lighting skills. I had to drag the picture together. I was the hatchet man.

But when he said that, he was having a sly dig at me too. Sometimes I'd say to him, 'You're over-rehearsing. The actors are getting stale', and he'd come straight back with, 'I'll rehearse as long as I like, Freddie.' 'Good for you,' I'd tell him. 'But time's getting on, you know. We're getting behind.'

There was a musical number with Ava and Elizabeth about how many husbands they'd had – nothing to do with the story, but for some reason George wanted it in. Ava had had a drink over lunch and kept forgetting her lines. After nine takes, the first and third were OK but the rest were getting worse and worse. 'God, George,' I complained, 'How much longer are we going on? We'll be here till Christmas!'

'All right, we will be here till Christmas, if that's how long it takes!'

'Well, I won't be!' I was speaking not so much for myself as for the unit as a whole. Everyone was fed up. This scene got cut from the finished film anyway.

During the filming of *The Blue Bird* Sydney Samuelson paid us a visit. George shouted across the set, 'You hear that, Sydney, isn't that a disgraceful exhibition? Since Freddie's arrived he's dominated the shooting, insulted me, taken over my job. I'm a broken man . . .' This from the man who told me to take over responsibility.

At the National Film Theatre George said, 'Freddie can be tough, but not me. I'm such a nice sweet person.' George was an old ham really.

People often said to me, 'You've been a successful cameraman for so long, haven't you ever felt you'd like to direct?'

The answer was yes and no. In a sense I had directed; I directed second unit on *Caesar and Cleopatra* as well as scores of training films for the army during the war. And on many other films I've been virtually co-director, when working with a director who was also acting, like Jack Buchanan or José Ferrer, or with an inexperienced director turning to his cameraman for guidance.

Of course there were times when I was sure I could direct the picture much better than the man who was in charge, and that was pretty frustrating, but on the other hand I also worked with some very fine directors. On the whole I didn't regret remaining a cameraman. In directing there's too much involved. You have to be a businessman. You spend months setting up a project, perfecting the script, arranging finance, negotiating with film companies, then at the last moment the whole thing collapses. As a cameraman you start work just before shooting, and when you've finished, that's it. You don't have these other worries. I've gone from one project to another, working all the time, whereas some directors in their entire career never make more than a dozen films.

Nevertheless, the idea of directing was always somewhere in my mind. On a couple of occasions in the 1950s MGM agreed to release me to direct a picture for another company, then they suddenly decided they needed me to light one of their own, and the moment passed. By the time I turned eighty, in October 1982, it seemed I'd left it too late.

That year I happened to meet David Puttnam. After his success with *Chariots of Fire*, winning the Oscar for Best Film, David was guest of honour at the annual BSC dinner. I was placed next to him at the table, and we got on very well. I suppose I must have mentioned that I'd always wanted to direct, because a short while afterwards I got a call from his associate, the producer Chris Griffin, asking if I'd like to photograph one of his 'First Love' films for Channel 4, a story about an old groundsman's love for his cricket field. Then Chris rang back. There had been a change of plan. Would I like to direct the picture?

I said yes straight away. There was no question in my mind that I could do it. I grabbed the opportunity with both hands.

Prior to shooting *Arthur's Hallowed Ground* my biggest responsibility was casting. The casting director sent along two or three actors for each part, and we – Chris Griffin, the writer Peter Gibbs and myself – interviewed them, asking them to read a bit of the script. After the session the three of us made our choice. I ended up with all the actors I wanted. A few days before shooting there was a read-through with all the cast. It was a wonderful session. I thought they were all great and I told them so. I felt absolutely elated.

At the beginning of May 1983 the unit – sixty-odd strong, including eleven actors – met in Coventry. Virtually the whole film was to be made at a cricket ground there. We had only twenty working days to shoot an eighty-minute film.

This is a normal situation. A director like David Lean can spend a year shooting a film, making every image and every detail perfect, but he's something of an exception. Producers allow that kind of latitude only to very few directors, those who have a solid record of box-office success. Normally one is under much more pressure to finish quickly. In my time I've worked with some very fast directors. One of the speediest was Richard Thorpe.

Dick Thorpe was the favourite director at MGM because he always finished on schedule. He made a point of it. The studio kept giving him a shorter and shorter schedule, but he always beat it.

On practically every picture I've made the producer has said at the beginning, 'We haven't got much money to do this, so we've really got to put our skates on.' They make a schedule, you read it through, and you think, this is really tight, God knows how we'll ever make it in that time. But by working overtime and slogging your guts out you just about manage it; perhaps with bad weather you might go a few days over. But what has actually happened is this: if the producers honestly and realistically work out the timing and it comes to twelve weeks, say, they will then schedule it for ten weeks so everybody feels they have to work terribly hard to keep to that schedule. That means if you finish in eleven weeks, a week over schedule, you're really a week *under* because it should have been twelve weeks in the first place.

But Dick Thorpe really would finish in ten weeks, or even nine. He had

Finally running the show! Freddie as director, with cast and crew of *Arthur's Hallowed Ground* (1983).

Stevie (1978): Freddie makes his point to Alec McCowan and Glenda Jackson.

a special method for working fast. On *Ivanhoe* he'd start with a long shot and keep filming until one of the actors fluffed. 'Cut!' Then he'd move the camera to a closer set-up. 'Come on, let's go. Action!' And shoot on until the next hold-up. 'Move in closer still. Continue!' And so on until we finished up with just two big heads filling the screen. In other words, the close-ups in the finished film were quite arbitrary, depending on the pure chance of the interruptions in shooting on that particular day. Thorpe never reshot anything. That's how he beat the schedule. For a cameraman it was boring as hell.

Working fast doesn't necessarily mean sacrificing finesse. *Stevie* (1978) is an excellent film about the poet Stevie Smith, but we shot it in only three weeks. Bob Enders, an experienced producer, was directing for the first time. 'I'm terrified,' he told me. 'I'm relying on you to help me out.'

'Don't worry,' I assured him. 'You've got a good team. It'll be OK.'

Bob left it to me and my operator, Chic Anstiss, to arrange the set-ups. Instead of doing laborious short takes, we devised a system of long takes. The conditions – mostly one set in a studio with a cast of four speaking parts – were ideal for that. When you have competent actors who remember their lines (Glenda Jackson and Mona Washbourne were recreating their stage roles as Stevie Smith and her aunt) you can zip along. The first day went extremely well. We did ten minutes and Bob was delighted. The next day was quite good too, with seven and a half minutes, but Bob was worried, he thought we were slipping. In fact, a five-minute average was all we needed to keep on schedule. With long takes one or two a day gives you at least that.

On *Arthur's Hallowed Ground* Chic was my cameraman. One way we hurried things along was in the way we did the master shot.

The master shot is a group shot of the whole scene done in one long take. The idea is to run straight through and give the actors a chance to work out their performances. Then you follow up with some close-ups, over the shoulders, singles. In most cases hardly any of the master shot is used – only perhaps the first ten feet and another bit towards the end – the rest being discarded during editing. Despite this, some directors will go on shooting the master shot, maybe fifteen times because in a long take there is more to go wrong, until they've got all of it right in the same take.

I handled it much more casually. If an actor fluffed I'd flick my fingers and say, 'Keep going. Go back a bit,' and tell the continuity girl to give the actors a cue two or three seconds back in the script. We'd carry on, not even cutting the camera, knowing the editor could sort it out later.

It's a very simple technique really, making a film, but some people make a hard job of it. They don't realize it's not necessary to get every take perfect so long as you get the part that you're going to use. If I'd had the chance to do another film, I wouldn't have shot as much as I did on this one. I wouldn't go right through the master shot, but just film the bits I needed and cut there. It's a waste of everyone's time end money and film stock to do take after take just because of one fluff in a part of the take that's not vital.

In shooting I tried to crack along as fast as possible. I said to Michael Elphick, one of the actors, 'I hope I'm not rushing you?'

'Not at all, Freddie. It's the way I like to work. It's boring hanging around.' All the actors agreed with this. I've noticed on other films how stale the actors get when they have to repeat the same take endlessly. On *Arthur* quite a lot of shots needed only one take; the most number of takes on a shot was six.

The weather was dreadful, the wettest May for years with only two sunny days in the three weeks, but we managed to adapt. A British cameraman has to become something of an expert on weather. On a cloudy day you need to be able to read the sky so you can say to the director, 'In five minutes the sun will come out and we'll have two minutes to get the shot in', and in this way take full advantage of the brief periods of sunshine available. There is a shot in *The 7th Dawn* in Malaysia, when Bill Holden walks across the street to Susannah York's sports car and at the very moment he opens the car door the heavens open and torrential rain pours down. At the end of the shot Bill said, 'That's amazing, Freddie. How did you do it?' Bill had made most of his films in the semi-desert climate of Hollywood. In England you get plenty of opportunity to acquire this sense of timing.

In the game of cricket bad light stops play, but film-makers can't always afford to wait for perfect light conditions. In Coventry we had a couple of brutes, and with these were able to make the cricket scenes look fairly presentable even on gloomy days.

It helped to be filming in just one location with all the actors present for the whole three weeks. That meant if we planned an exterior scene and it rained, we moved indoors and filmed an alternative scene in the club secretary's office, the committee rooms, the massage room. On any given day the actors' call sheet told them to expect a variety of scenes, depending on circumstances.

In the lead was Jimmy Jewel, an old comedian who became a fine straight actor. Before we started he told me, 'My memory's not what it used to be. I'm not sure I'll be able to remember my lines on some of the longer speeches.' In the event he needn't have worried. Jimmy's entertainment background came in useful in another way. We had borrowed an old motor roller from Rugby School for a flashback sequence. When the time came to use it, the damn thing wouldn't start. It defeated six experts for a couple of hours. Meanwhile we were busy shooting another scene elsewhere in the grounds. Jimmy said, 'Let me have a look at it.'

A quarter of an hour later the engine coughed to life.

'Before the war,' Jimmy told us, 'I bought an old Model T Ford for £500, and I turned it into a trick thing. It would cough and splutter; it could go round the stage on its own; a door would fall off. I became a complete expert on the Ford. And this roller here has the same engine.'

In March 1984 *Arthur's Hallowed Ground* was shown at the National Film Theatre to an audience that included thirty or so groundsmen. They were thrilled and delighted. In the film, Arthur's wife remarks, 'You're married to this ground.' One of the groundsmen told me, 'I daren't let my wife see this film, because that's what she's always saying to me.' They loved some of the details, such as the groundsman resenting cricketers stamping on his beautiful turf, the bowlers criticizing the groundsman because the pitch is so perfect they can't turn the ball on it. Like most people, they had the idea the director was responsible for everything – the conception, the research, the writing. 'What made you think of it in the first place?' I was asked. I told them they'd better talk to the writer, Peter Gibbs, a former county cricketer who wrote the original story.

Epilogue

Arthur's Hallowed Ground turned out to be my final film credit, although I carried on making commercials until I was eighty-five. In 1982 I lost the sight of my right eye from glaucoma, which I kept quiet about, fearing producers wouldn't have much confidence in a one-eyed cameraman. I used to squint through the eyepiece of the camera with my left eye, but no one seemed to notice.

When I retired I immediately went back to painting. Over the years I've done several hundred, with almost a hundred of them hanging in my flat. I was given an exhibition at BAFTA once.

Reunited: *Lawrence of Arabia*'s main players on the occasion of its restoration in 1992.

The newly honoured Dr Young celebrates his doctorate from the Royal College of Art, with his wife Joan.

In 1992 *Lawrence of Arabia* was relaunched. When the film first came out, Sam Spiegel made David cut it by twenty minutes so exhibitors could show three screenings a day instead of two. It was a thrill seeing the original, longer version, restored by Bob Harris. Joan and I attended the première in New York, along with David Lean, Martin Scorsese and Steven Spielberg. Spielberg told me it was seeing *Lawrence* in 1962 that decided him to seek a career in films. We went on to attend special screenings in Washington and Los Angeles, then on to Cannes for the festival.

Some months later I was invited by Christopher Frayling, the Pro-Rector, to speak to his film students at the Royal College of Art. The RCA now has a Freddie Young scholarship for one student a year, thanks to the £70,000 raised by Michael Samuelson, who tragically died in 1998 and is sorely missed. Michael was simply a 'one-off'. For my ninetieth birthday he hosted a marvellous party at Pinewood Studios, which was attended by practically every member of the BSC. Later, in July 1994, the Royal College of Art honoured me as Doctor of Art, which I thought not bad for someone who left school at fourteen.

I fell and broke my hip a couple of years ago, which slowed me down and tied me more or less to a wheelchair. I keep in touch with a few old

'I've just been incredibly lucky': Freddie Young at home.

cameramen like Freddie Francis and Ossie Morris, and I go to the BSC dinners once a year.

I often wished I'd had a better education, but on the other hand I have travelled all around the world at someone else's expense. Directors of photography have better equipment these days, more sophisticated lights, faster stock. So many of the visual effects are done digitally in post-production. They can put another actor's head on somebody else's body; if a road is macadamed, they can make it gravel; if they shoot a street scene with unwanted television aerials, they can make those aerials disappear. So, in a way, a lot of creativity has been taken away from the cameraman whereas in our day we had to do it all in the camera. You had to use your imagination. Now, looking back just after the centenary of cinema, I think I worked during the best years of the film industry.

I worked in the industry for seventy years, photographing more than 120 films, being paid to do something I love. If I hadn't been a teenager in Shepherd's Bush, living just down the road from a film studio, it might all have been different. At the age of ninety-six I look back and I think, I've just been incredibly lucky.

Afterword

The movie-going public will remember Dad for his work, but those of us who knew him will remember him also, and most importantly, for the sort of person he was.

I will remember Dad for his energy. I was often asked what it was like to have an old Dad. The truth is, it was only in the last few years that Dad showed his age. Once, he was called at 4.15 a.m. for an early shoot. He was a little breathless, and he apologized for his delay in answering the door: he'd just been doing some press-ups. He was 82 at the time.

I will remember Dad for his honest, unexaggerated re-tellings of film-making stories. As you can imagine, Mum and I got to hear these quite a few times; and it would have been easy for him to play the fisherman, whose prize catch gets bigger with each re-telling of the tale. But Dad wasn't like that – all his wordly success and acclaim never affected his essential character.

I will remember Dad for his modesty, even his touching lack of confidence at times. Around 1988, he was presenting an award at a grand ceremony. Afterwards, he confided to Sydney Samuelson that he hadn't made a brilliant job of it. Sydney said, 'Freddie, you were the only one who was natural.'

I will remember Dad for his courage, particularly in adversity. In the last couple of years Dad suffered from increasing disability and pain, but he never complained. During his last time in hospital, his spirit was just as evident. After prodding him with numerous needles, the doctor said to Dad, 'I'm sorry for hurting you.' Dad immediately replied, 'Not half as sorry as I am.'

Above all else, it is Dad's gentleness and his love that I will remember him for. His legacy will live on, not only on the screen, but also in our hearts, and in the way in which we seek to emulate those qualities of his that we most admired.

David Young

Filmography

As second cameraman:
1927 The Flag Lieutenant (Maurice Elvey)
1928 The Somme (M. A. Wetherell)

As director of photography:
1928 Victory (M. A. Wetherell)
Bluebottles (Ivor Montague)
The Cure (Ivor Montague)
Daydreams (Ivor Montague)
1929 White Cargo (J. B. Williams)
1930 The W Plan (Victor Saville)
The Sport of Kings (Victor Saville)
A Warm Corner (Victor Saville)
1930 A Peep Behind the Scenes (Herbert Wilcox)
Rookery Nook (Tom Walls)
Plunder (Tom Walls)
Canaries Sometimes Sing (Tom Walls)
On Approval (Tom Walls)
Tons of Money (Tom Walls)
1931 Tilly of Bloomsbury (Jack Raymond)
The Speckled Band (Jack Raymond)
Carnival (Herbert Wilcox)
The Chance of a Night Time (Herbert Wilcox)
Mischief (Jack Raymond)
Up for the Cup (Jack Raymond)
The Loves of Robert Burns (Herbert Wilcox)
1932 Goodnight Vienna (Herbert Wilcox)
It's a King (Jack Raymond)
Leap Year (Tom Walls)
The Love Contract (Edwin Knopf/Harold Selpin)
Thark, Turkey Time (Widgey R. Newman)
The Mayor's Nest (Maclean Rogers)
1933 A Night Like This (Tom Walls)
Summer Lightning (Maclean Rogers)
Yes, Mr Brown (Herbert Wilcox/Jack Buchanan)
Bitter Sweet (Herbert Wilcox)

The Little Damozel (Herbert Wilcox)
Just My Luck (Jack Raymond)
The King's Cup (Herbert Wilcox)
Night of the Garter (Jack Raymond)
A Cuckoo in the Nest (Tom Walls)
Up for the Derby (Maclean Rogers)
1934 The Blue Danube (Herbert Wilcox)
That's a Good Girl (Jack Buchanan)
Trouble (Maclean Rogers)
1935 Girls Please! (Jack Raymond)
Nell Gwyn (Herbert Wilcox)
Peg of Old Drury (Herbert Wilcox)
Come out of the Pantry (Jack Raymond)
1936 The Queen's Affair (Herbert Wilcox)
The King of Paris (Jack Raymond)
Two's Company (Tim Whelan)
Fame (Leslie S. Hiscott)
The Frog (Jack Raymond)
Limelight (Herbert Wilcox)
1937 When Knights were Bold (Jack Raymond)
London Melody (Herbert Wilcox)
Victoria the Great (Herbert Wilcox)
Millions (Leslie S. Hiscott)
1938 The Three Maxims (Herbert Wilcox)
The Rat (Jack Raymond)
Sunset in Vienna (Norman Walker)
Sixty Glorious Years (Herbert Wilcox)
This'll Make You Whistle (Herbert Wilcox)
A Royal Divorce (Jack Raymond)
1939 Goodbye Mr Chips (Sam Wood)
Nurse Edith Cavell (Herbert Wilcox)
1940 Busman's Honeymoon (Arthur Woods)
Contraband (Michael Powell)
1941 49th Parallel (Michael Powell)
1942 The Young Mr Pitt (Carol Reed)
1945 Caesar and Cleopatra (Gabriel Pascal)
1946 Bedelia (Lance Comfort)

1947 While I Live (John Harlow)
      So Well Remembered (Edward
      Dmytryk)
1948 Escape (Joseph L. Mankiewicz)
      The Winslow Boy (Anthony Asquith)
      Edward, My Son (George Cukor)
1949 Conspirator (Victor Saville)
1950 Treasure Island (Byron Haskin)
1951 Calling Bulldog Drummond (Victor
      Saville)
1952 Giselle (Henry Caldwell)
      Ivanhoe (Richard Thorpe)
      Time Bomb (Ted Tetzlaff)
1953 Mogambo (John Ford)
      Knights of the Round Table (Richard
      Thorpe)
1954 Betrayed (Gottfried Reinhardt)
      Invitation to the Dance (Gene Kelly)
1955 Beyond Mombasa (George Marshall)
      Bedevilled (Mitchell Leisen)
1956 Bhowani Junction (George Cukor)
      Lust for Life (Vincente Minnelli)
1957 The Barretts of Wimpole Street
      (Sidney Franklin)
      The Little Hut (Mark Robson)
      Island in the Sun (Robert Rossen)
      I Accuse (José Ferrer)
1958 Gideon's Day (John Ford)
      Indiscreet (Stanley Donen)
      The Inn of the Sixth Happiness (Mark
      Robson)
1959 Solomon and Sheba (King Vidor)
1960 Gorgo (Eugene Lourie)
      Hand in Hand (Philip Leacock)
      Macbeth (George Schaefer)

1961 The Greengage Summer (Lewis
      Gilbert)
1962 Lawrence of Arabia (David Lean)
1964 The 7th Dawn (Lewis Gilbert)
      Lord Jim (Richard Brooks)
1965 Rotten to the Core (John Boulting)
1966 Doctor Zhivago (David Lean)
1967 The Deadly Affair (Sidney Lumet)
      You Only Live Twice (Lewis Gilbert)
1968 Sinful Davey (John Huston)
1969 Battle of Britain (Guy Hamilton)
1970 Ryan's Daughter (David Lean)
1971 Nicholas and Alexandra (Franklin
      Schaffner)
1972 The Asphyx (Peter Newbrook)
1973 Luther (Guy Green)
1974 The Tamarind Seed (Blake Edwards)
1975 Great Expectations (Joseph Hardy)
      Permission to Kill (Cyril Frankel)
1976 The Blue Bird (George Cukor)
      The Man in the Iron Mask (Mike
      Newell)
1978 Stevie (Robert Enders)
1979 Bloodline (Terence Young)
1980 Rough Cut (Don Siegel)
1981 Ike and the War Years (Boris Sagal,
      for TV)
      Richard's Things (Anthony Harvey)
1983 Invitation to the Wedding (Joe
      Brooks)
      Sword of the Valiant (Steven Weeks)

As director:
1983 Arthur's Hallowed Ground

Index

Figures in *italics* refer to captions